UP TO YOU, INC.
www.depressed-letstalk.com
Sturgeon Lake, MN

Ten Essential Facts of Life Every Teenager Should Know

By Dan Celentano

Edited by Michelle E.C. Henriques
Illustrated by Dave Kirwan

Dan Celentano Books
UP TO YOU, INC.
Sturgeon Lake, MN
Printed in the United States of America

Dan Celentano
UP TO YOU, INC
44192 Pioneer Road
Sturgeon Lake, Minnesota 55783

Printed in the United States of America by Arrowhead Printing,
Inc.

First Edition ©2003 by Dan Celentano.

ISBN 0-9709495-2-9

To my friend, J.C.

TABLE OF CONTENTS

INTRODUCTION

The following pages contain
ten essential facts of life every teenager should know.

No lectures.

No preaching.

Just telling it like it is on the ten facts of life.

What more can be said?

That's why the title of this book is

TEN ESSENTIAL FACTS OF LIFE
EVERY TEENAGER SHOULD KNOW.

Pretty smart, huh?

Well, maybe not.

When you come to a
point in your life
where you must choose
between
right or wrong,

ask yourself a very
important question first...

F A C T   O N E

I'm about to make a choice.

Do I want the choice I'm going to make
to turn around
and
end up making me?

If you learn one thing from this book,
learn what is called

THE ULTIMATE TEENAGE SAYING.

It could save you a *multitude* of problems in life.

THE ULTIMATE TEENAGE SAYING
goes like this:

YOU ARE GOING TO MAKE CHOICES IN YOUR LIFE, AND THE CHOICES YOU MAKE WILL ALWAYS TURN AROUND AND END UP MAKING YOU...

EVERY TIME.

Sounds simple enough, right?

Well, you'd be surprised at the number of
teenagers who just don't get it; especially those
people who repeatedly make bad choices or those
who make choices that are clearly just plain dumb. To
them, there's no such thing as being accountable for
bad behavior.

Take the two girls who recently appeared on the
NBC Nightly News for example.

One of the girls in this story was 15 and the other was 16 years old:

The 16 year old tried to convince her friend to rob a convenience store. After a short time, the 15 year old reluctantly agreed to do it.

The older girl got her father's handgun and both girls headed for the store. In the store, the surveillance cameras recorded the 16 year old holding a gun on the cashier while the other girl looked out for the cops. The girls got the money and both headed out the door.

Shortly after, you could see on the surveillance tape a police car with its red lights on racing across the front of the store.

Both girls got caught and eventually ended up in front of a judge. After a short lecture on the bad choices they had made, the judge sentenced the girls to 7 years in prison. Not juvenile hall, but *prison*.

After hearing the sentence, the 15 year old fainted in her lawyer's arms. The lawyer struggled to hold the girl up to prevent her from falling to the floor. The other girl was crying uncontrollably.

The judge then said to the girls,

"You know, I have to say, I really don't feel sorry for you. In fact, if I could have given you 10 years, I would have given you 10 years. But I can only give 7. Take them out of here."

As they were both being led away, you can see the judge lower her head and slowly shake it as if to say...

"What the heck were those girls thinking?"

To be honest,
when I saw this on the news I didn't feel sorry for them either. They made the choice to rob the store and the choice turned around and made them.

What's the problem here?

Why did the one girl faint?

Why was the other girl crying uncontrollably?

What did they think was going to happen if they rob a convenience store?

This example of
THE ULTIMATE TEENAGE SAYING
can apply to anything:

from sex to messing around with your education;
from doing drugs to drinking.

Before you do something that can really have a *major*
negative impact on your life, ask yourself if
you want the choice you're about to make
to end up making you.

If you say "no" and stop yourself from making
a bad choice, you've saved yourself a multitude of
problems like I said.

If, on the other hand, you don't really care what
happens and you go ahead and make the bad
choice anyway,
you can always tell yourself

while sitting in jail,
or
in a drug rehab center,
or
in a doctor's office waiting for a pregnancy test,

or *wherever...*

"You know, I wish I hadn't done that."

FINAL THOUGHT

The bottom line to this chapter is simple:

Whether you end up in jail
or
end up in college,

do drugs
or
do the right thing,

have sex
or
have self control,

no matter what the situation may be,

You are going to make choices in life
and
the choices you make,
good or bad,
will eventually end up making you. ...

...Some will "make you" for a lifetime.

F A C T   T W O

*Making bad choices
is the number one reason
teenagers find themselves
in trouble.*

*The friends they
hang out with are the
number one group
of people who influence
the bad choices they make.*

Are you a **STREET PUPPET**?

STREET PUPPETS are people who feel that the only way they can ever be accepted by anyone is to just go along with "the crowd" when "the crowd" wants them to do something wrong.

-To a **STREET PUPPET**, it really doesn't matter how dangerous this act may be, or how painful it may be to their family or how embarrassing it will be to themselves, **being accepted** is all that matters.

-To a **STREET PUPPET**, you don't "make waves" by saying "*no*" to something even though **you know** it's wrong.

-To a **STREET PUPPET** there exists no courage **within** to **stand alone** when a situation comes up that might really "mess up" the person for years to come.

-To a **STREET PUPPET**, you just...... **go along** with everyone. Being accepted to a STREET PUPPET is that easy. Just......**go along** with the crowd. Never mind what may happen as a result of your actions, just........ **go along**.

Well, truth is **being accepted** is easy but you don't have to "**just.....go along**" to have people "hang out" with you. (**FACT #10** will show you why.)

Anthony sure didn't understand this.

Anthony's Story is true and it's a good example of how easy it is for some people to get trapped into becoming a STREET PUPPET to begin with.

Anthony was a slender 16-year old boy who never thought he'd find himself in the kind of trouble he was in. After all, he had never even been sent to the principal's office much less to juvenile jail.

As he stood looking out the narrow window from his cramped jail cell, Anthony kept asking himself the same questions over and over again:

"What am I doing here? How did I get into this mess? How could I let this happen?"

Anthony's problems started when his family moved from North Carolina to a small town in Minnesota. He was new to his high school and wanted very much to be accepted.

One day, a small group of boys came up to Anthony and asked him if he wanted to go to a beer party that evening. Never before in his life had Anthony gone out drinking.

He didn't like the taste of the stuff and never saw a need to do something he didn't like just to hang out with friends.

But because he wanted to be accepted in his new school, Anthony put aside all of that for now and agreed to go to the party.

At the party, Anthony drank just one can of beer. Even that was tough for him to take.

But drinking just one can of beer didn't stop Anthony's "friends" from asking him to go to another party.

He went to that party and drank. Then to another party and drank. And to still another party and drank.

It got to the point where Anthony wasn't drinking just one can of beer anymore.

He was drinking a six-pack, some vodka, and some rum.

Anthony liked hanging out with his new friends even though they did things that were totally against what he believed in.

Hanging out with these people gave Anthony a sense of importance, of acceptance—like he was

SOMEBODY to SOMEBODY.

This also gave Anthony a feeling of security: something he had never had before in his life. There were people around and if it took drinking to make this happen, so be it.

In time, Anthony actually believed that the people he was hanging out with were the kind of friends who would be there for him if he ever really needed them.

There was, however, a down side to this whole situation.

Anthony couldn't see it at the time, but it wouldn't take long for him to discover what it was.

You see, the boy who'd never been drinking before, who had always tried to do the right things in life, who had put aside his values just to be accepted, was now developing a drinking problem.

Anthony was at a point where he would drink just about anything his friends would put in front of him.

But, like I said, having a drinking problem was the last thing on Anthony's mind.

Little did Anthony realize that when friendship is built upon sand instead of rock, it doesn't take long before the rain washes it away.

And the rain in Anthony's life was about to come down and come down hard.

It all started on a Saturday evening, 2 days before his birthday.

Anthony went to one of his parties thinking nothing of it. Just another party to him.

When he walked into the house, he saw his "friends" sitting in a circle on the living room floor. Not giving any thought to it, Anthony sat with them.

Shortly after he sat down, someone pulled out a marijuana cigarette, lit it up, took a drag and then passed it on to the next person. This person also took a drag...and so on.

The marijuana was eventually passed to Anthony.

Everyone waited for him to take a drag. He stared at the joint for a moment, then raised his head and slowly moved his eyes around the circle. As he was doing this, his mind began to race.

"I don't want this garbage," he thought. *"Drinking is starting to mess me up enough. Like I really need something else to make it worse? Forget it!"*

He then passed the joint to the next person without taking a drag.

"*What's the matter?*" one boy said in a sarcastic tone, "*Too strong for you?   Want a candy joint instead?*"

Everyone in the circle laughed.

"*Give me a break, kid!*" another said to Anthony. "*I didn't think you were such a baby!*"

Suddenly an uneasy feeling crept into Anthony's body. As he looked around, the faces he once knew were no longer familiar, but rather dark shadows of people he had never met before. This made Anthony feel really uncomfortable—so much so that he wanted to leave.

But as Anthony tried to stand up, something peculiar happened. He couldn't seem to get off the floor; it was like he was glued to the carpet.

The heavy hand of possibly being rejected literally held Anthony in place. He was afraid that if he left that party, people would make fun of him, and no one would ever want to hang out with him any more.

So he stayed. The marijuana kept going around and Anthony kept passing it on. The more he did, the more uneasy he felt.

Suddenly there was a knock at the door.

"Open up," a voice on the other side said. *"It's the police. We got a complaint of too much noise. Open the door."*

As everyone scrambled to try to get away, the front door slammed open and the police came in arresting everyone for possession of a controlled substance.

As Anthony was being handcuffed, he turned to his friends for support.

"What's up? Someone tell them I didn't do nothing. Come on! Tell them I didn't do nothing!"

Anthony expected his friends to speak up for him. He actually expected someone to cover his back. But no one said anything. Some just looked away while others smirked.

"Come on!" Anthony said in an anxious voice. *"Quit messing around! You know I didn't do anything. Tell them! Tell them!"*

Once again, silence. The only thing that could be heard was the clicking of handcuffs.

Anthony slowly hung his head. A look of anger and frustration showed on his face as he was led out the front door.

All that time wasted, he thought. *All that time thinking that those creeps were my friends. Man, what a sucker I am.*

And what do I have to show for it?

A pair of handcuffs, a drinking problem... and a bunch of coconuts I thought were my friends.

≈

After serving time at the Hyland Detention Center for probation violation, Anthony was sent to an alcohol treatment facility to get help for his drinking problem.

But Anthony's Story doesn't end there.

Shortly after, his family moved again—this time to a town in southern Minnesota.

Anthony was new to this high school and wanted to be accepted. However, after all he's been through, he was now a lot wiser. And it didn't take long for him to put this wisdom into action.

One day, a boy from the "in crowd" came up to Anthony's locker and invited him to a beer party.

Anthony paused.

He raised his head, looked the boy squarely in the eye and said in a slow, soft but firm voice, *"A beer party? I don't want to go to your beer party..."*

Another pause.

"...And if you're smart," he said as he put some books in and closed his locker door, *"you don't want to go either."*

~

The point of this story is simple.

If the friends you hang out with don't respect you first as a person,

chances are good that they are going to either

USE YOU

or

LOSE YOU.

**If you don't believe it now,
believe it when you see it.**

I think Anthony finally understood this.

Hope you do too.

THE ULTIMATE FRIENDSHIP TEST

Did you ever wonder why the people you
hang out with
hang out with you?

I mean, do they hang out with you because they
like you as a person,
or
do they hang out with you for some other reason?

Want to find out?

Take

THE ULTIMATE FRIENDSHIP TEST

and see for yourself.

Here's how it works...

Hang out with your friends as usual.

Mess around,
have a good time,
enjoy your friendship with them as
you normally would.

After all, they're your good friends.

However, if any of your friends want you
to do something that could really mess you
over in some way—serious things like
drinking,
stealing,
drugs,
skipping school,
or whatever—
do the right thing instead.

Don't walk away from their friendship,
just simply do the right thing.

Give some reason why you don't want to do it
and
tell them you'll call them later.

After two weeks of doing this, look around.

Who's left?

Who's still hanging out with you?

Who still calls and stays in touch with you?

Whoever they may be,
they are people
who hang out with you because they have more
*respect for you as a **person***
than for anything else.

Keep them, because they're not bad friends to
have around.

No matter how you look at this test,
whether you think it's
dumb,
old fashioned,
or wouldn't think of taking it
because you're afraid of what you might find out,

the bottom line never changes when
it comes to friendship.

That is,

RESPECT
and
true friendship
are
INSEPARABLE.

FINAL THOUGHT

The

ULTIMATE FRIENDSHIP TEST

is a great test for dating, too.

Especially if the topic of sex ever comes up.

Enough said.

Who is the toughest person in your school?

A. *The biggest, "baddest" football player on the team?*

B. *The school bully?*

C. *A boy named Mike Tyson?*

D. *Someone who eats glass for lunch?*

E. *The "outsider" or the kid in your school no one else talks to or wants to be seen with?*

**F
A
C
T**

**T
H
R
E
E**

The answer is "E."

The toughest person in your school
is the person other people perceive to be
the weakest.

They are the people who hang out on the fringes of
acceptance, but never seem to be able to
cross the line.

They are the ones who get
put down by others,
get picked on by bullies
and
are ignored by all those
who think they are "too good"
to associate or be seen
with someone who is

"not their equal."

What makes these people so tough?

To answer this question you only have to put
yourself in their position.

If, throughout the school day, you
get picked on by bullies,
put down by "wanna-be's"
and are ignored by everyone else,
wouldn't you have to be a pretty tough person
to handle all of this and still keep an air of
SELF RESPECT about you? You sure would.

To be sure, it's something the name caller,
the bully
and the conceited person
would all have a hard time doing.

(See for yourself what it's like to be put in a
position like this by reading
"Andy's World" on page 39.)

My advice to the "outsider" is simple:

Hang in there.

You'd be smart not to let other people change you
from being who you are
to the kind of person THEY expect you to be.

Fact is,
sooner or later someone is bound to realize
that there's a lot more to you than just
the "label"
other people put on you.

If it hasn't happened already, it surely will.

One of the best kept secrets in the world
is just how tough
the so-called loner or "outsider"
really is.

Well, it's no secret anymore.

THE UNDERTAKER

I took a group of kids to watch a professional wrestling match at the invitation of a friend who is the manager of the arena where the match took place.

Toward the end of the match, my friend asked me if I wanted to take the kids to meet one of the wrestlers. I asked the kids, and without hesitation, they all enthusiastically said yes.

It was then that we were all taken down to an empty room to wait for a wrestler named the UNDERTAKER.

Also waiting in the room was a sickly, skinny, frail-looking nine year old boy sitting in a wheelchair with his mother standing by his side.

Before long, this giant of a man appeared in the doorway. It was the UNDERTAKER. He was ugly and he was big. In fact, he was so big that he had to duck to get through the frame of the door.

Shortly after he entered the room, the UNDERTAKER spotted the little boy in the wheelchair and slowly walked over to him.

The poor boy was so intimidated by this huge man that he began to physically shake as the wrestler came closer to him.

You could have heard a pin drop in that room as the UNDERTAKER approached the wheelchair. Everyone was waiting to see what this wrestler was going to do.

Knowing that this man made his money by projecting a fierce image, I think everyone was waiting to be entertained by him.

I'm sure the kids who were with me were all expecting him to speak to the boy in an intimidating voice. Something like,

"I am the Undertaker and I will drop-kick you if you mess with me!!!!!"

If he did this, everyone would have understood that this was the role he played and no one would have thought twice about it.

No one except the little boy in the wheelchair.

Had the UNDERTAKER done such a thing, there's no telling how this frightened, sickly child would have reacted.

However, the UNDERTAKER did not do this.

Instead, he knelt down on one knee next to the boy, put his arm around him, snapped his fingers and had his manager bring over an UNDERTAKER t-shirt.

The UNDERTAKER took the T-shirt, gently laid it on the boy's chest, patted it down to smooth out any wrinkles, and then patiently waited for him to react.

The boy, however, could not stop shaking and soon the shirt folded from his chest down to his knees. The wrestler—contrary to his image—patiently and gently picked up the shirt, put it on the boy's chest, patted it down and once again waited for the boy to react.

Eventually, the little boy began to respond. He looked down at the t-shirt and then very slowly—almost reluctantly—turned his head to look at the UNDERTAKER. With some hesitation at first, the boy forced a smile as his body gradually stopped shaking.

The UNDERTAKER, sensing the time was right, gently pulled the little boy toward him and gave him a hug.

The boy was in *heaven*. It had to be the most exciting thing that ever happened to him. He was resting his head on his hero's chest. Man, things couldn't get any better than that.

The point of this true story is simple:

*The hero in the room that day was **not** a professional wrestler.*

The hero in that room was the man behind the wrestler.

Here's a man who could have easily put on a show by intimidating the little boy. Like I said, no one would have thought twice about it. Instead, the UNDERTAKER chose to respect and embrace the boy.

This story reminds me of some of the people in your school. The true heroes in your school are not necessarily the athletes or the most popular kids.

Fact is, the true heroes in your school are the people who respect those who everyone else disrespects.

Why are they heroes?

Because in the process of respecting those who are
being disrespected they realize that they may be
criticized for it, yet they still go ahead
and do it anyway.

And anytime someone risks their life or their
reputation to benefit others, that person is a hero.

The UNDERTAKER knew that if he stepped out
of character he could be criticized for it and even
tarnish his image. But yet he still went ahead and
did it anyway just to benefit that little kid.

The UNDERTAKER earned more respect from
the people in that room that day than he could
have ever earned wrestling in the ring.

He certainly earned mine,
and I don't even watch wrestling.

~

Did you ever wonder what it would be like
to be an outcast in your school?

What's it like to go to school day after day
where the only people who will talk to you are
the teachers?

Even if students do talk to you, they talk to you
not out of friendship, but out of
temporary politeness.

Maybe the following story can help give you just
a small idea on how it would feel to be in
this position.

The story is fictional, but you can bet the events in
the story are real.
It happens to thousands of teens every day.

When you read the story, try hard to put yourself in
Andy's position.

If you do, you'll understand what I mean when I say
people like Andy are, without a doubt, the toughest
people in your school.

Welcome to
ANDY'S WORLD

"We as human beings are given only
"one pair of shoes" in our lifetime
and are never allowed
to walk in another."

"Mrs. Corbi. Mrs. Corbi, your son is awake. You can go in and see him now."

Mrs. Corbi slowly opened her eyes, momentarily stared up at the doctor, then quickly got up and rushed into her son's room. Not knowing what she'd find, she reluctantly walked in and then gently sat in a chair next to her son's hospital bed.

"Dominic," she whispered. "Dominic, it's Mom. How are you feeling?"

Dominic slowly opened his eyes and turned his head toward his mother. "I'm all right, Ma," he said. "Don't worry. I'm all right."

There was a noticeable silence before his mother spoke up again. "Dominic, you sure you're all right?"

Dominic turned his head away. Tears began to slowly stream down his face as he blankly stared into space.

"Dominic, look at me. What's wrong? You hurt somewhere? Want me to get the doctor for you?"

"No, Ma, don't. I'm all right," he said while turning back to face his mother.

"If you're not in pain, Dominic, then why are you crying?" she asked. "Let me get the doctor for you."

As Dominic wiped the tears from his face, he looked directly into his mother's eyes and made a startling statement.

"I have to tell you something, Mom, but I don't know where to begin. I don't understand it myself."

"Dominic, what are you talking about?" his mother asked.

"Mom, just listen and try to believe me." Dominic's mother backed off a bit. "Go on, Dominic," she said, "tell me what you're talking about."

Dominic adjusted his body to get more comfortable. Raising his eyes to look at his mother, he began to tell an extraordinary story:

"Well, ya see, it's like this..."

~

One day in school Willy, Robert and I were hanging out in the hallway waiting for our next class to start when we saw Andy coming down the hallway.

You got to understand this kid, Andy, Mom. Andy's kind of an outcast in our school: a loner. As long as I've known him he's had only one friend and that was when he was in like the 6th grade. But that kid moved away a long time ago. I've never seen him hang out with anyone since.

We picked on Andy now and then, but we didn't really mean anything by it. We were just having some fun. Nobody thought it was a big deal.

Anyway, when Andy saw us, he turned and tried to walk the other way but we caught up to him.

Robert started going through his back pack looking for I-don't-know-what while I started to mess around with his glasses. He kept trying to pull away telling us to leave him alone but we kept messing with him

Eventually, Robert had his book bag and I had his glasses.

We were just fooling around with him, Mom. We didn't mean no harm or nothing.

After we started messing around with him Mr. Williams, the janitor, stepped in to break it up.

He made me give back the glasses and made Robert give back the book bag. Andy was mad. He grabbed the glasses and book bag and I didn't think nothing of what we did to him.

To me, it was just another day of fooling around with Andy.

After the janitor made me give back the glasses, he called me into an empty classroom.

"Don't you think you guys have picked on that boy long enough?" he asked me. "Day after day you pick on that kid. Why?"

I remember telling him that we were just having some fun with him and that nobody was getting hurt or nothing. I also remember telling him to lay off. "You're only the janitor," I said, "so just back off."

After I said that, Mr. Williams looked at me. "You'd be surprised who I am, kid," he said. Before I could ask him what he meant by that, he went on with what he had to say.

"You say you're not hurting anyone—that you're just having fun with him. But did you ever look at it from his side? Do you really know what it's like to be in his shoes?"

I told him to knock it off with all that sweet talk and just leave me alone.

Then something strange happened. He walked toward me a little bit. I backed off thinking he was going to hit me or something.

Instead, he looked me dead straight in the eye and said, "Maybe, just maybe, you should know what it's like to walk in his shoes. Maybe you'd think differently if you did."

Then he said something that made me really think. He said,

"After all, we as human beings are given only 'one pair of shoes' in our lifetime and are never allowed to walk in another. You, my friend, need to walk in another."

Even though I thought this guy was crazy, I will still never forget those words. I don't know why. And the way he looked at me. The man scared the heck out of me.

As I began to walk away, I stopped and turned around to see if he was still looking at me. But when I did, he was gone. It was like a bolt of lightening went through my body. "Where did he go?!" I asked myself.

I tried to brush it off thinking maybe he went out the back door or something, but there was no back door.

That night, while I was in bed, I thought a lot about what Mr. Williams said and especially that look he gave me. I couldn't get those piercing eyes out of my mind.

And those words:

"We as human beings are given only 'one pair of shoes' in our lifetime and are never allowed to walk in another. You, my friend, need to walk in another."

What did he mean by that? It drove me crazy. I was up half the night thinking about it.

Then it happened.

~

Dominic paused a moment. His face suddenly began to turn white as he stared out in space.

"Dominic," his mom asked in concern. "What's the matter? You all right?"

Dominic slowly turned to his mom.

I know you're not going to believe me, Mom. But just try, all right? Please, just try.

"Dominic, I'll believe you," his mom said. "Just tell me what happened."

Dominic paused once again. He seemed to be debating as to whether he should continue with the story.

After a few moments, he went on.

≈

The next morning, I was awakened by some girl.

"Andy," she said, knocking on the bedroom door, "Andy, get up. Time for school."

I opened my eyes right away. After staring at the ceiling a bit, I turned my head to look around the room.

What I saw made my heart beat really fast. It wasn't my room. I was sleeping in someone else's bed in some strange room.

"I began to panic. I sat right up in bed. Just then,

there was another knock at the door."

"Andy," this girl said, "are you up? Come on, you have to tend to Dad."

I couldn't move. I sat frozen. I thought maybe this was all a bad dream or something. That maybe if I went back to sleep I would wake up in my own room. But it wasn't a bad dream. It was more like a nightmare.

I pulled the covers off of me and got out of bed.

As I began to walk around the room, I kept asking myself, "Where am I? What is this place?"

Then I turned and looked into the large mirror that was on the dresser. What I saw scared the heck out of me. My legs became so weak I had to hold on to the dresser to stop myself from falling to the floor.

≈

"What did you see?" his mom asked.

Dominic paused briefly before he answered.

"Dominic, what did you see?" she asked again.

"I—I saw Andy." Dominic said looking straight ahead as though he were hypnotized.

"Andy?" his mom asked.

"You don't gotta believe me, Mom, but I'm telling the truth. I saw Andy. I couldn't believe it myself. I thought I was freaking out or something, but there I was. I was in Andy's body."

~

After looking at myself for a while, a knock came to the door again.

"Andy, you up? Come on! You're gonna be late!" the voice said.

I didn't know what to say or do.

"Andy? You hear me?"

"Yeah," I finally answered. "Yeah, I'm up!"

"Andy," she said, "I'm coming in." Just then the door swung open. I saw this girl who looked like she was in her 20's brushing her hair.

"Come on! You're not even dressed for school," she said while brushing her hair. "Hurry up. You have to give Dad his pills."

Then she left the room. I stood there for a moment trying to understand what was going on. I kept telling myself that it was all just a bad dream.

Soon after, I started to get dressed. My legs were so weak I could hardly stand. I put on a pair of Andy's jeans, a shirt, his socks and black and white sneakers.

After I got dressed, I went to the door and slowly peeked around the corner. I was scared to death. As I was peeking around the corner, the girl called up to me from downstairs.

"Andy, I'm leaving for school now! Dad's pills are on the end-table. Hurry up or you'll be late." Just then the front door slammed shut and there I was all alone in this strange house and in the body of another person. I didn't know what to do.

I went back into the room and looked into the mirror one more time. Maybe everything would be back to normal. Maybe I was Dominic again. Maybe this dream would be over. But no such luck.

As I looked at myself in the mirror, I slowly ran my fingers across my face to see if I was real. I was. For some strange reason, I was in Andy's body.

Just then the words of Mr. Williams came to me...

"We as human beings are given 'only one pair of shoes' in our lifetime and are never allowed to walk in another. You, my friend, need to walk in another."

"Could it be?" I thought to myself.

"Naaaa, this is just a dream," I said, "Don't worry, you'll wake up soon."

Then I decided to go downstairs. As I walked through a hall that led to the stairs, I noticed some pictures on the walls. They were mostly of Andy and his family. I think it was his mom, dad and the girl who woke me up.

When I got downstairs I looked around a bit. I went into the living room and was amazed at the number of family pictures there were: the family at the beach, the family at Disney World, the family at Christmas, family this, family that. You didn't have to be a genius to realize that this was a close-knit family. Just by looking at the pictures, you knew that these were people who really cared about each other.

There was one picture I picked up of Andy and his dad together. Andy must have been about 5 years old. I couldn't help but notice how Andy was looking at his father; like he was his hero or something.

I remember this picture because it was the way I remember that picture because it was the way I looked up to Dad. I must have looked at that picture for like 3 or 4 minutes.

As I was putting the picture down, the front door suddenly flung open. It was Andy's sister. "I forgot my history book," she said rushing up to her bedroom to get it.

When she came down from getting her book, she went to a room not too far from where I was standing. She opened the door and walked in. "Andy," she called out to me, "did you give Dad his pills yet?" I didn't know what she was talking about. Pills? What pills?

Although I didn't really want to go in that room, I was still curious about what was in there. When I walked in, I saw a man laying on what looked like a hospital bed. His eyes were shut, and there was like a plastic tube sticking out of his arm that was hooked up to some bottle on a stand near the bed.

As I got closer to the man, I realized it was the same man I had seen in those pictures. It was Andy's father. I later learned from Andy's sister that he was dying from cancer. When I was told this, I imagined the picture I had been holding in the living room, the one of Andy and his father, falling to the floor and breaking into pieces.

"Did you give Dad his pills?" his sister asked me again.

Once again, I didn't know what to say.

"Andy, did you give Dad his pills?" she asked me for the third time.

Not knowing what she was talking about, I just told her that I didn't.

She handed me some pills to give to her father but then changed her mind. "Never mind," she said, "why don't you go on to school. I'll give them to Dad and wait for the day nurse to come."

I stood there for a moment not knowing what to say, how to act or where to go. I was all confused.

"Go to school," she said again. I turned to leave but before I did, I looked back. I felt really bad. I not only felt bad for his dad and sister, but for Andy too.

I rushed off to school that day hoping someone would recognize me. Maybe this whole nightmare would finally be over.

As I walked in the front door of the school and headed down the hallway, I started to say "hi" to people I knew, expecting them to say "hi" back to me. But that didn't happen.

Some of the people I said "hi" to looked at me strangely. Some turned their heads away from me. Others ignored me, hoping their friends didn't hear me. Still others just looked straight ahead like I didn't even say anything. There were a few people who said "hi" back to me but you could tell that they were just trying to be nice and that was about as far as it went.

It didn't take long for me to realize that I was in Andy's body and Andy wasn't exactly the most popular kid in school. As I walked down the hallway, all I could see were people looking through me as though I didn't exist. It was like I was invisible or something.

It was a strange feeling for me. I felt like I was at a party and all the people there were strangers. As Dominic, I never had this happen to me before.

Then I saw Linda, my girlfriend, getting something from her locker. I was like, "Finally! Someone who will know me—somehow, some way, she will know who I am."

I went up to her locker and just stood there hoping by some miracle she would recognize who I was. She slowly turned to look at me.

"Andy," she said in that nice soft voice she has, "do you want something?" I figured I'd say something that would kind of jog her memory so she'd know who I was.

"Yeah," I said to her, "I just wanted to know if you had a good time at the dance last week." Linda stood there staring at me like I was some kind of nut.

Then she said something like, "Yeah, Dominic and I had a real good time. Is there anything else you want, Andy? I have to get to class."

I was really disappointed. No way she was going to recognize me. I shook my head and told her there was nothing else I wanted. She closed her locker, looked back at me with a strange look and then walked away. I wanted to tell her it was me so bad, but I figured it wouldn't do no good.

I remember thinking that all wasn't lost in talking to her. At least I learned that she had a good time at the dance with me.

I waited for a few more moments at her locker hoping she would come back and tell me she was just kidding, that she knew it was me all along, but she kept right on walking away.

As I turned to leave, I bumped into some old friends. It was Willy and Robert. At first I was happy. They were my best friends. How could they not recognize me?

"Hey, guys! What's up?" I said. I quickly learned that recognizing me wasn't going to happen.

"Get away from us, you little knot-head," Robert said.

Then all of a sudden *he* came around the corner. I couldn't believe my eyes.

~

Dominic paused for a moment from telling the story. "Who was it, Dominic?" his mom asked.

Dominic pointed to his chest. "*Me*," he said. "It was *me*. I was looking right into the eyes of myself. Here I was in Andy's body looking at myself!

"You can't imagine what it's like looking at yourself from somebody else's body. I was paralyzed with fear. I remember asking myself, "What's going on here? How could this be happening?"

~

Just then Dominic grabbed me by the ear and pulled me toward him. Having myself by the ear was the strangest feeling I ever had in my life. I had *me* by the ear!

"You got me in trouble yesterday, you little punk!" Dominic said to me. "I ought to kick your butt right here and now—but I won't. I'll get you some other time. Bet on it."

My glasses were all crooked on my face from the force of Dominic pulling me toward him. I looked at him with fear. I was really scared. Not only couldn't I believe that was me, but the anger in his eyes scared the heck out of me.

I never knew I could be like that.

Soon my ear began to really hurt. I was starting to get mad so I told Dominic to get off me and quit messing with me. He pushed me away, stared at me for a moment and then all three boys started to leave.

Before they left, Robert knocked my books to the floor. I stood there for a moment looking at those guys.

I was really angry. I didn't know whether to jump on them, curse them out or just leave it be.

As I bent down to pick up my books, the people passing by me were bumping into me like I wasn't even there. A few stepped on my books, some pushed me aside and one kid even cursed at me telling me to move out of the way.

No one, not one person, tried to help me.

It was like someone threw some trash on the floor and it was just in the way of people passing by. I was the trash. I was so ticked off, I wanted to curse everyone out. I wanted to knock down everyone's books and have them feel what I felt. I wanted them to know what it was like to be treated like this.

But I knew I couldn't do anything. This made me even more angry. "Punks!" I said to myself, "Dirty punks!"

Just then, the bell rang for the first period class.

I stood there in anger for about like 5 minutes looking down the hallway before I headed to my gym class.

Being in gym all these years as Dominic, it was a common thing to have students pick teams to play a game. And you know I'm a good basketball player, so I was always expecting to be the first one picked and usually was.

That day, we were playing basketball so I figured there would be no problems.

But then I realized I wasn't in Dominic's body. I was in Andy's skinny little frail-looking bony body. This presented a whole new set of problems for me.

One by one, I watched as my classmates were being picked ahead of me by the two captains. There went Tom, Rene, Richard... Elizabeth.

Eventually, I was standing there alone. I felt weird. I was never put in a position like this before. I never knew how it felt to be picked last until now.

And it wasn't just being the last one picked that bothered me; it was the attitude of the captain doing the picking that made me feel stupid.

When the person before me was picked and the captain realized I was going to be on his team, he said to the teacher, "Ahh, man, do we have to have him on our team?"

There I was standing in the middle of the floor all alone. I felt like there was a big spotlight on me showcasing the school dummy. Everybody was looking at me, some even laughing at what the captain said. And I couldn't do anything!

I remember hanging my head a little. I felt so humiliated.

For much of the game, all I did was run up and down the court. No one would throw me the ball. While I was running, I felt awkward, clumsy. Once or twice I even tripped over my own feet. Then I remembered that it wasn't me who was running down the court, but Andy.

Funny, I always thought that everybody liked sports and that everybody could play them. It didn't take long for me to realize that this wasn't the case.

Toward the end of the game, someone finally threw me the ball. Actually, the person who threw it was being triple teamed and had no where else to throw it but toward me.

When the ball was thrown to me, it slipped out of my hands and into the hands of a player on the other team. The kid who grabbed the ball went down the court and scored a basket.

My teammates jumped all over me like I was the only player who ever made a mistake in the whole game.

When I—as Dominic—played basketball, I made a lot of mistakes during a game. Nobody ever said anything to me then. Not one thing.

Needless to say, the ball never came my way again during the rest of the game.

When the class was over and everyone was leaving the gym, I felt like everyone was looking at me; like everybody was blaming me because we lost the game.

I played a lot of basketball as Dominic, but I was never so glad to see a game end than I was with that one.

For some kids, school is a place to not only learn, but to also hang out with friends.

As I went from class to class that day, I began to realize there wouldn't be any friends for me; there wouldn't be anyone for me to talk to. I was all I had. Do you know how hard it is to go through school all day with no one to talk to but the teachers?

Soon it was lunchtime.

When I got in line, a few kids tried to cut in front of me. I started to get angry. I tried to defend myself by pushing my way back into the line but the more I pushed, the more they pushed back. I just wasn't strong enough to defend myself from the people who were trying to cut in.

Suddenly, I felt a tug on my arm. It was Mr. Burnstein, the Assistant Principal.

"What's going on here?" he asked me. I told him that people were cutting in front of me in line. The kids who were cutting all denied it and said I was the one trying to cut in line.

No one in line would dare stick up for me. God forbid if their friends ever saw them sticking up for Andy! There were like ten other kids there and not one person said anything.

Believing the three or four kids who tried to cut in, Mr. Burnstein pulled me by the arm and put me in the detention room for the lunch period. Someone eventually brought in my lunch tray.

Sitting there by myself in the room, I stared at my food as I picked at it with a fork. I was so frustrated! I started crying. I remember the tears dripping onto my glasses and then onto my food. "Creeps!" I said to myself, "They're all creeps."

As time went on, I found out that when I did get my lunch, I would end up sitting at a table by myself. Seemed like no one wanted to be seen with me.

It was like I was some kind of freak who had to be kept separate from everyone else because there was something wrong with me. I never felt so all alone in my life.

Sometimes there would be no empty tables available, so I had to sit at a table where there were like two or three other kids already sitting. When I sat down I felt very uncomfortable. I would slowly put down my tray not knowing how the people at the table would react. I would look at the people, sort of like asking them for permission with my eyes to sit down.

The kids would look at each other with smiles on their faces and would say very little. The smiles weren't one of those "just trying to be nice" smiles. They were smiling as if to say, "can you believe this kid? He's got some nerve sitting here. Who does he think he is, sitting with us?"

Soon after I sat down, the kids would all get up and leave.

After school, I started to walk home. My home. But then I thought you wouldn't recognize me, Mom. I figured you'd call the cops on me or something because this strange person was in our house. I decided to go back to Andy's.

As I walked in the door, I saw Andy's sister coming out of her father's room. I asked her how "Dad" was. She hung her head a bit and asked me to join her in the living room.

She told me that it didn't look good for Andy's dad. I guess she was preparing me for his death or something.

Even though he wasn't my father, I was really sad. I hung my head. I don't know why, but it really bothered me. I never felt bad for anyone in my life before.

After I got the news about her father, we both got to talking. I didn't exactly like being in Andy's body, but I was still curious to learn more about his family.

I found out that Andy's sister was a college student studying to be a lawyer. I was so anxious to learn stuff about the family, I began to ask what I now realize were dumb questions. Questions like "where's your mother?"

When I asked that question, Andy's sister gave me the strangest look. She asked me if I was feeling okay. I told her I was fine.

"You know what happened to Mom. Why would you ask me a stupid question like that?" she answered.

I remember there was a strange silence after she said that.

"You miss Mom?" she asked me. I didn't know what to say. I couldn't answer.

Then she gently took my hand and said, "It's okay, you can tell me. It's okay to miss her. I think of her all the time. I will never get over the accident; I will never get over her death. I miss her so much."

The sad tone in her voice is something I will never forget.

First news about her dad, and now this. I felt really bad for this girl and especially for Andy. I remember asking myself, "how much more can this kid take?"

Then I realized something. Andy's close-knit family was the one place he could go to with his problems. It was his place for the love, attention and respect he didn't get from anyone else. Now he only had his sister for this; his mom and dad were gone.

I hung my head again. I remember whispering to myself, "I'm sorry, Andy, I didn't know." I felt like the mean school bully you see on TV that everyone hates.

Let me tell you something: it's one thing to hear about how tough someone else has it, but another thing to actually go through that person's experience for yourself. I was finding out what it was like to actually go through Andy's hard times.

It wasn't pretty.

Morning after morning I would wake up, quickly sit up in bed and look around the room hoping I'd be home again. But I wasn't.

Day after day it was the same old thing: the disrespect at school, the depression at home, the loneliness. It seemed like there was no escape.

After a few days, going through the halls in school and seeing other kids messing around with each other, walking together, talking about what they were going to do after school and the parties they were going to attend made me want to be a part of it all in some way.

But as long as I was Andy, that wasn't going to happen. As Dominic, I knew what it was like to have friends. As Andy, I knew what it was like to have no one.

After school, I began to develop a routine. I'd put my books on the end table and go up to Andy's room. I'd close the door and go to a corner of the room and just sit on the floor with my knees pulled up against my chest. I would sit there feeling angry, frustrated, depressed, lonely and confused. Man, I never knew I had so many emotions.

One day while I was sitting on the floor, I remembered the necklace Dad gave me before he left home for good. I wanted to hold that thing. I don't know why; I just wanted to hold it.

Andy and I had something in common. I too knew what it was like to go through hard times at home.

However, I didn't know what it was like to have all this other stuff at school get poured on top of it. It was like getting tackled really hard in a football game, laying there in pain and then having ten other players jump on top of the pile.

I wonder if Andy sat in that room thinking about all that went on in his life. Maybe he sat in the very spot I sat in.

Then it happened.

I was in the bathroom in school one day and was just about ready to leave when Dominic, Willy and Robert came in. I never could get used to seeing myself face to face. I especially could not get used to the way I acted.

I tried to leave the bathroom but they wouldn't let me go by.

Then, without any warning, they all grabbed me and turned me upside down while trying to put my head in the toilet. I fought and fought but couldn't get them off of me. "Knock it off!" I kept yelling, "Knock it off!"

"Just then, someone came in. Lucky for me. Even though it wasn't a teacher, they still let me down. I was so close to being totally put into the toilet that the top of my head was wet.

"That's what you get for getting me in trouble the other day, you little nerd," Dominic said as they all left the bathroom laughing at what they did.

There I was sitting on the floor by the bathroom toilet. I felt dirty. I felt humiliated. Tears were running down my face. All that had been going on and now this. It was the lowest point in my life-as either Dominic or Andy. I wanted to get those punks, one of which was me. I wanted to get them so bad!

I quickly got up off the floor, left the stall and flung the bathroom door open. I rushed down the hallway and out of the school on my way to Andy's house. I can't tell you how angry I was. The anger took over my whole body.

As I came closer to the house, I noticed that there was an ambulance parked out front. I walked up the porch steps where Andy's sister greeted me at the door. She gave me the news that Andy's father had died.

I can't explain why, but I lost it. I just broke down and cried.

Maybe it was because of all the frustration and anger that had been building up inside of me. Maybe it was because of the guilt I felt for all the trouble I caused Andy as Dominic. Maybe I related it to when Dad left home. Maybe it was just because I was getting to know and love this family and my heart went out to them. I don't know why. All I know is, for some reason I broke down and cried.

I didn't think I had anymore tears left in me, but I guess I did. I remember ending up on the floor of the porch on my knees bent over crying uncontrollably.

Andy's sister gently lifted me off the floor, wrapped her arms around me and cried along with me. I couldn't stop crying for about like 10 minutes. Was it Andy crying or was it me? It could have been both of us.

~

Dominic paused a few moments from telling the story to wipe away tears from his eyes. Then, staring into space, he continued.

~

Once I got a hold of my emotions, I slowly turned and walked off the porch. I just had to be alone. I remember Andy's sister calling out to me saying, "Andy, where are you going? Andy!" I kept walking.

I was in a daze; like I was hypnotized or like I was walking in my sleep or something. Everything that had happened to me in the past few days was just too much for me to handle.

As I walked down the street, I kept asking myself the same thing over and over. "What have I done to this kids? What have I done?"

At one point, I was stopped by some old man. "You all right kid?" he asked me. I slowly looked up, stared at him for a moment, and then kept walking. I could say nothing.

It was then that it happened.

I came to a street corner and instead of stopping, I kept walking. Shortly after I stepped off the curb, I heard a car honking at me. I turned to look and before I could react I was hit in the arm and thrown backwards onto the ground. I remember laying on the ground for a few minutes until I passed out.

The next thing I remember is waking up here in the hospital.

That's it, Mom. That's the whole story. You wanna believe me, good. If not, fine. But that's the whole story and it's true.

~

Dominic paused a moment. Silence filled the air as his eyes slowly lowered in deep thought.

He then glanced over at his mother to get her reaction. She just stared at him in amazement.

She slowly leaned back in her chair, took a deep breath, thought for a moment, then gently leaned forward once again.

"Dominic," she said in a soft voice, "Dominic, you were having a bad dream. That's all it was. It was just a bad dream. Maybe the medication the doctor gave you had something to do with it. It was just a dream, Dominic."

"No!" Dominic insisted, "No, it wasn't a dream." Dominic's mother stared at him for a moment, looked up at the doctor and then back at her son.

"Look, Dominic," she said while putting her hands on his shoulders and gently pushing him down onto the bed, "the doctor says you need to get some rest. Why don't you lay back and get some sleep, all right? Everything is going to be all right. That's a good boy."

When his mom did that, Dominic felt like a 4 year old kid who came in from playing outside and told his mom that he was Superman and that he just got back from saving 100 people from a burning building. In other words, there was no way Dominic felt that she believed him.

Dominic's mom got up from the chair and went over to the doctor. "Maybe you should get some counseling for him or something," he said. "This boy might need some help."

Dominic looked over at his mother. He then turned his body to face the wall. "Don't need no counselor," he said to himself. "Don't need no counselor."

Dominic then thought about all that happened.

"I'm Dominic again. I escaped. But Andy is still there. He will be there his whole life. The only chance he has of escaping is if people understand where this kid is coming from. Will people in my school take the time to understand? Those creeps? They're all too worried about their own reputations to care about anybody else.

I always thought I was tough enough to handle anything. But just after a few days, I was the one who couldn't take anymore. I was the one who was weak.

Who's the tough guy now, Dominic? Who's the tough guy now?"

~

The day finally arrived when Dominic was to leave the hospital. Anxious to go home, he was up early.

He got out of bed and quickly began to get dressed.

As he was getting dressed, he glanced up to see a man mopping the floor outside of his hospital room. Thinking nothing of it, he continued to dress. When all his clothes were on, he looked around for his sneakers.

"My sneakers..." he said to himself, "where are my sneakers?"

Looking everywhere, he couldn't find them.

Then a strange thing happened. The man who was mopping the floor came into the room holding a pair of sneakers.

Dominic looked up and gasped, "Mr. Williams? What are you doing here?"

"Mr. Williams?" the man answered, "who are you talking about kid? I just came in to see if these were your sneakers. They were sitting outside the door here. Are they yours?"

With a fearful look on his face, Dominic's eyes slowly lowered from the man's face to the pair of sneakers he was holding.

"Yeah," he said in a guarded voice. "Yeah, they're mine"

"Are you sure?" the man asked.

"Of course I'm sure. They're the only pair I own."

"Well, then," the man told Dominic as he handed the shoes over to him, "they must be yours if they're the only pair you own."

Then the man said something to Dominic that sent a chill through his body.

"You know what they say about having only one pair of shoes, don't you?

"Ahhh, let me see, how does that go again...?

"Oh, yeah. 'We as human beings are given only "one pair of shoes" in our lifetime and are never allowed to walk in another.' Yeah, that's it. That's what they say. Did you ever hear that saying before?"

Dominic was in shock. He hesitated a moment before he answered. "Yeah," he said while looking at the man in disbelief, "yeah, I heard that before."

Dominic then slowly walked toward his bed and sat on the edge to put his shoes on. He never took his eyes off the man, that is, until he bent down to tie them. When he finished, he looked up only to discover that the man was gone.

"Ahhhhhhh, maaan," he said stomping his foot on the floor, "Not again!"

Dominic quickly looked around the room and saw a hand mirror lying on the end table. He reluctantly lifted the mirror up to his face to see who would be staring back at him.

Touching his face, he saw his own reflection.

He breathed a sigh of relief, put the mirror back on the table and then went to the door to see if "Mr. Williams" was still around.

He wasn't.

Shaken by what just happened, Dominic slowly returned to his bed and sat down.

Shortly after, his mother came through the door. "Hi, Dominic. Ready to go?" she asked.

Dominic's eyes were still focused on the door. "Yeah," he said, "yeah, I'm ready. Let's get out of here. Quick."

"Is there something wrong, Dominic?"

"You're not going to believe this, Mom," Dominic answered, still looking out the door. "but..." Just then Dominic stopped talking and turned to look at his mother. "Never mind," he said slowly shaking his head. "Never mind, let's just go."

Mrs. Corbi looked at her son strangely. "You know, Dominic," she said as they walked out of the door, "your first appointment with the counselor is on Monday. You won't forget, will you?"

Dominic quickly turned to look back at his room. "Don't need to no counselor, Ma," he said as he turned back again to look at his mom. "Don't need no counselor."

As they walked down the hallway and past the janitor's room, a man slowly stepped out and leaned up against the door jam. He folded his arms and smiled as he watched Dominic and his mother walk down the long corridor that led to the front doors of the hospital.

EPILOGUE

After Dominic got out of the hospital, he made numerous attempts to talk to Andy. But Andy wanted no part of it. He simply didn't trust Dominic and who can blame him?

But Dominic was determined to prove himself.

He finally got his chance one Tuesday afternoon when he found Robert and Willy messing around with Andy in the gym locker room.

To make a long story short, it would be the last time those two even came close to Andy again.

Soon after, Dominic and Andy became friends and hung out together often.

From this point on Willy and Robert wanted nothing more to do with Dominic because of his friendship with Andy

This wasn't a problem for Dominic.

Maybe, just maybe, all those two guys need is a little "janitorial care."

If you know what I mean.

As you saw with Andy, no one knows what a person goes through in life. You only see a small portion of a person's day at school. What goes on the rest of the time? Something to think about before you pick on someone who is either physically or mentally weaker than you are.

Better yet,
maybe you should think about why you would see a need to pick on someone who is weaker than you in the first place. A lot of people say it's because the bully is so insecure about him or her self, that he or she needs to **bring other people down** just to **build themselves up**.

Maybe that's why the bully only picks on those people he or she perceives to be weak instead of strong. After all, it's hard to build yourself up if you're always "getting knocked down" by someone who is stronger either physically or mentally.

I think this is what is meant by the saying...

*"Those who bully the weak
are weak before the strong."*

When the day comes in which you, the bully, are standing in front of **"the strong,"** I hope **"the strong"** you're standing in front of will have **compassion**, **not contempt**, for you, the **"weak."**

FINAL THOUGHT

True story from Connecticut... A 16-year-old boy who has a rare form of dwarfism; he was a little over 3 feet tall and weighed only 42 pounds, asked a girl to go to a school dance with him. The girl turned him down. Could the reason she turned him down be because her reputation was on the line? Maybe, maybe not. It really doesn't matter. Fact is, another girl, a very pretty girl who probably could have gone out with most any of the guys in her school, stepped up and told the boy she would go with him. Both went out and had a good time.

"It was the happiest day of my life," he said. *"It showed I was appreciated. I was really happy."*

By his own admission, the boy doesn't have very many friends, and considering the fact that the doctor only gives him maybe 10 or so more years to live, happy moments like this can't come often enough.

~

Now a days it seems as though athletes rule when it comes to defining who a hero is. I guess there's nothing wrong with that. However, understand this; A person who is a hero because of his or her athletic ability usually effect others for as long as the athletic ability lasts. A hero like this girl effects others for a lifetime.

~

Can't think of a better way to summarize this chapter.

Time to tell it like it is about sex.

FACT FOUR

You can read what you want to read,
see what you want to see,
hear what you want to hear,
or
believe what you want to believe.

But the fact is, the true meaning of sex
has always been,
still is,
and
always will be the same.

That is...

Sex is the highest form of expression for the love a man and woman can show for each other.

There's touching.
There's holding hands.
There's kissing.

But sex expresses,
in the highest form possible,
just how much a man and woman love each other.

It should be the kind of expression of love
you would want to save for someone
you are ***totally*** committed to—

committed as in
marriage.

That's right: *marriage.*

Yeah sure, I know what you're probably thinking.

"Marriage?

What are you nuts?

This is the 21st century.

You don't need to be married to have sex nowadays."

And you'd be right...

...that is
if you're the kind of person who doesn't mind
being *used* by other people.

I'm sure you've all heard about how people get
used by others in reference to sex...

but did you ever understand *why*?

It's simple...

When you get married, basically what you are
saying is this:

*"Out of all the people in the world, you are the
one person I want to spend the rest of my life with.
I love you that much
and I want to express to you, in the highest form
possible, this love I have for you."*

Sex is the ultimate expression of that love.

When your girl or boyfriend tells you that they want
to have sex with you because they
"love you",
do you really believe that this is the kind of love
they're talking about?

If you do, you're living in a FANTASY LAND
and sound very much like the eight girls
I interviewed on this very subject.

Each one of these eight teenage girls
I talked to had a baby,
and each one,
without exception,
said the following:

"I thought my boyfriend loved me for me.
At least he said he did.
Later though, I found out that this wasn't true."

Maybe the reason the girls felt this way was because seven of the eight girls never saw their boyfriend again.

Then I asked the following question:

"If your boyfriend loved you as much as
he said he did, don't you think he would
have respected your decision
not to have sex?

I mean, wouldn't this kind of respect for you as
a person be more of an indication of
his love than just jumping into bed with you?"

There was an eerie silence for a moment.

Then one of the girls spoke up...

"I don't know how he would have reacted
if I said "no."

I would hope he would have respected my decision,
but to tell the truth, I don't know."

You can take the following statement
to the bank and either
save it, deposit it, or cash it in... .

*Any person who wants to have sex with you, who is
not totally committed to you as a person,*

*is someone who is also not totally committed to
another person he or she is having sex with.*

In other words,
you're **being used**, just like all the other people
the person sleeps around with.

It is something to think about before you jump into
bed with someone who says,

"I love you."

Speaking of being used by people,
there are some teenagers who feel pressured
into having sex because they don't want
to have the stigma of

"being a virgin"

attached to them.

They feel that having sex is a way to earn the
RESPECT of others.

These are people who feel that RESPECT comes
from **what you do in bed,**
as opposed to **who you are as a person.**

Fact is,
having a reputation for sleeping around
won't earn you the respect of others,
but more likely will attract other people
who will also want to use you.

Fact # 1
sums up the issue of teenage sex very well.

That is, before you make the choice of having sex,
ask yourself the following question.

"I am about to make a serious choice.
Do I want the choice I'm about to make
to turn around
and
end up making me?"

If you don't mind the consequences that may occur
from your actions,
what more can be said?

If, on the other hand, you're not ready to take on
responsibilities such as having a child or catching
some sexually transmitted disease,

or

if you simply don't like the fact that you're
being used by other people,

then it would be wise to show a little

SELF CONTROL.

I'm sure that the eight girls I interviewed wished they had taken this advice before they jumped into bed with someone who said,

"I love you."

By the way...

There was one other thing the girls I interviewed
said that you might find interesting.

Each one,
without exception,
said that they thought the baby
they were going to have
would give them the love and attention
they never got at home.

This brings up a question:
Could many of the sexually active teenagers today
be searching for the love they
never received at home?

Taking this question one step further,
if a person believes in their heart that no one
could ever love them enough to ever be committed
to them, will they really care if they're being used?

I'm not so sure.

However, I do know this:

Looking for love with the wrong people
won't fill the desire a person has
to be loved.

Finding someone who is absolutely
committed to you will.

(**The Search For Shelby** story on **page 181** can
show those who are interested where you would
need to start looking for this person.)

To put this another way:

Love can wait to give.

But lust can't wait to get.

FINAL THOUGHT

I received the following email from a girl through my website, www.depressed-letstalk.com. I asked her if I could use it in this book.

I can't think of a better way to summarize this chapter.

~

I lost my virginity at 14 years old.

I met this guy my freshman year; we really were not good friends before we started dating. It all happened so fast. A month into our relationship I thought he loved me, and I loved him and we'd be together forever. We spent all of our time together.

During this time I was struggling through depression and lots of other problems in my home life. Then I decided to have sex with him. I thought it was out of love; that this would really bring us closer and we'd have a better relationship. I thought "hey since he's having sex with me and telling me he loves me, then he must love me."

We were together for six months all together.

A few times I thought I was pregnant. My mom had always told me never to have sex at such a young age because nobody is emotionally ready. Well I never believed her. Then all he and I ever did was just have sex, all the time. I thought this meant good.

Then he ended it. He began smoking pot, and we would fight. He ended it, and I really couldn't believe it.

I mean I really, really thought he cared about me.

From then on I have NEVER been the same. I got really depressed. I felt used and abused. I felt so many emotions and anger. I wanted to kill him for lying to me.

I am still living with the decisions I made, which were the wrong ones. I just sat there and cried and cried. I can't believe I let someone take my whole body and just destroy it all. If only I had listened to my mom when she said sex at a young age is so emotional for someone to handle at this age.

Man was she right. It all haunts me still after months have passed.

In the end, we never talk anymore, and actually he's in jail. Nobody at such a young age is ready for what sex will bring you.

Please just listen to my story and really think about it. It's so powerful and emotional and you really don't know this until it all ends the way you never thought it would. But I have living proof that it WILL happen.

Thanks,

Brenda C.

F
A
C
T

Other than a lack of
desire to be the best
and
an unwillingness to
prepare,

Fear of Failure

is the major reason
why some teenagers
don't succeed at
reaching their goals
in life.

F
I
V
E

There are teenagers reading this book right now
who could be GREAT athletes.

No doubt about it.

There are some who could easily get
straight "A's" in school.

There are still others who could be
GREAT performers.

Many teenagers have the ability to achieve
greatness and reach the goals they set for
themselves, but at the same time, many of these
very same people won't even come close to
realizing their potential.

It's not because they don't have a strong desire
to be the best at what they do
or
that they are not willing to put in the time it takes
to prepare.

It's because some teenagers suffer from
what is called a

FEAR OF FAILURE.

A FEAR OF FAILURE surfaces
when a person works toward reaching a goal
in life, and then suddenly stops at a point
far short of the goal he or she is trying to reach.

Why would a person do this?

Why would a person who could be great
at something not allow him or herself to
follow through on reaching
this greatness?

To answer these questions, consider
the elephant in the circus...

Why does the elephant in the circus,
the most powerful animal in the world,
have only a rope attached to his leg to hold him?

Won't he break the rope and get away?

He certainly could if he wanted to.

Why not a chain or something stronger?

The answer is simple.

When the elephant was a baby, the circus owners attached a big, heavy chain to his leg to hold him.

Every time the baby elephant walked, the chain would tighten up. Thinking he could break the chain and free himself, the elephant would violently yank at it.

**After all,
no one has ever told him he couldn't break the chain.**

When the elephant realized that breaking the chain wasn't possible, he'd turn around, walk in another direction and try it again, only to have the same thing happen.

Every time the elephant would yank at the chain and try to break free, his mind would become a little more **conditioned into believing** that he's limited as to how far he can go.

The elephant would walk, the chain would tighten up, the elephant would yank at it, and while he was yanking at it, his mind would tell him,

"You can only go so far, **so quit trying**."

At first the elephant doesn't believe this and keeps yanking at the chain.

However, after a few days when the elephant would walk, the chain would tighten up, the mind would kick in and the elephant would begin to believe that maybe it's true.

"Maybe I can only go so far."

It doesn't take long for the elephant to finally become totally convinced that he can only go a short distance. Soon, he won't even make an effort to yank at the chain anymore.

Instead, the elephant would walk, the chain would tighten up, the mind would automatically kick in telling him he couldn't do it and without even trying, the elephant would simply turn around and walk the other way.

The elephant has now been conditioned to believe that no matter how hard he tries, he can only go so far. The circus owners can now take off the chain, put on an inexpensive rope and save themselves a few thousand dollars in the process.

People who suffer from FEAR OF FAILURE
are much like the baby elephant.

As they were growing up, they too had a "heavy
chain" put on them by the people around them who
would constantly give the message that

they are only so good
and
can only go so far in achieving anything they
set out to do in life.

After many years of receiving this message,
their minds become conditioned to believe that
they are limited as to what they can do.

So every time these people start to
approach greatness and reach the goals
they set for themselves,

their conditioned mind kicks in that they are only
so good and can only go so far.

Much like the elephant, they eventually

"back off, turn around
and
go the other way,"

never reaching their full potential.

It's like the Chinese Proverb says:

A man who tries to catch 2 rabbits at the same time will catch neither.

In other words,
you can't work at being successful at something
while at the same time focus in on your
FEAR OF FAILURE.

One "rabbit" has to go.

It's up to you to decide which one.

For those who suffer from FEAR OF FAILURE,
there's a constant battle going on in the mind.

First, there's the desire to want to
achieve greatness and reach the goals
they set for themselves.

Then there's

the chain that holds them back from achieving
their goals.

Unfortunately, the mind is automatically focused
more on the chain than it is on the goals.

Therein lies the key to turning this around.

The more a person focuses on
the goals they're working on,

the looser the chain becomes.

The reason for this is because people who have
been conditioned all of their lives to fail are
conditioned to focus only on their failures and not
on achieving their goals.

Turn this line of thinking around, and things are
going to change for you.

One more suggestion that will help you with a
FEAR OF FAILURE
can be found in Fact #7.

Read it carefully because without it, all the focus
in the world won't help.

FINAL THOUGHT

Someone once said...

*"Failure is the frightful thing you see
when you take your eyes
off of your goals."*

Need I say more?

F A C T   S I X

*The hardest thing for
teenagers to understand is
this...*

*Problems
an individual may have
do not fall on the lap
of other people,
unless other people
let it happen.*

This chapter is addressed to all the teenagers who blame themselves for family problems they have absolutely nothing to do with.

Believe me,
this is a bigger problem than you may imagine and one that can be really destructive to an individual.

To start off with, let me give you
the bottom line
to this chapter...

*Respect for family is **essential.***

*Keeping family problems which have
nothing to do with you
separate from your personal life
is **crucial**.*

That being said,
let me make my point by asking you
a few questions about the following three stories.

One

Rachel's mom is an alcoholic. She's been in for treatment a number of times but has not kicked the habit. In treatment, it was discovered that Mom had a very troubled past that led to her drinking.

It's quite obvious that mom's drinking problem had nothing to do with Rachel. How could it? But try convincing Rachel of this. For one reason or another, Rachel can't help believing that she had something to do with it; that she must have done something wrong.

Question...

Should Rachel feel guilty about her mom's drinking problem?

If not, then whose problem is it?

Why?

Two

Tom's parents recently got a divorce. Long before Tom was born, his parents had problems. They often fought and rarely got along with each other.

Tom blames himself for the divorce.

As in the case of Rachel, he too feels guilty— thinking that maybe he had something to do with it.

Question...

Should Tom blame himself for his parents' divorce?

If not, then whose problem is it?

Why?

Three

Karen's stepfather has been physically abusive to her from time to time. He flies off the handle at the littlest things. He has had this anger problem a long time, even back to when he was a child.

However, Karen believes that the reason her stepfather hits her is because of something she did and not because her stepfather has a problem. Because of this, she sees herself as having little value.

Question...

Should Karen blame herself for her father's anger towards her?

If not, then whose problem is it?

Why?

It should be quite obvious what the answers are to
all of these questions;

**_Problems an individual may have
do not fall on the lap of other people
unless other people let it happen._**

Can't put it any plainer than that.

But try convincing certain teenagers of this. Fact is,
it's the hardest thing for a teenager to understand.

The same teenagers who would answer
the previous questions with no trouble at all,
are some of the same teenagers
who would turn around and blame themselves
for the very same thing.

Teenagers are notorious for doing this.

In many teenagers' minds, parents or other relatives
never had any problems before they came along.

*"After all, they are our parents or uncles or aunts or
whatever. How can they have any problems?..."*

...And if their parents or other relatives didn't have
any problems before they came along,
then it's safe to say it must be their fault when
problems do come up.

Does this sound right to you? Well, if it does, then I
hate to say it but you're living back in
FANTASY LAND.

Don't get me wrong. It's like I said:

Respect for family,
especially for you parents,
is essential.

They brought you into this world,
took care of you and love you
more than you will probably ever know.

However, fact is adults do have
personal problems like anyone else,
and yes,
sometimes those personal problems do fall on
other people.

Intentionally? No way. However, some teenagers
DO let it happen.

That's just the way it is.

For you people who blame yourself for all your family problems, you'd be smart to understand that not all problems fall under one category.

This is especially true when it comes to family problems. Truth is, there are two types of family problems:

Problems you have control over
and
problems you don't.

(Yes, as much as you may not want to believe it, there are some problems *you don't have control over.*)

For those problems **you do** have control over, problems *caused by you* and ones *you can solve* if **you choose to do** so, such as
curfew,
school work,
doing drugs,
respect for parents,
getting to school on time...

you must do what you have to do to make sure you take care of your own business.

These kinds of problems rest on your shoulders and are ones you need to take responsibility for.

For the problems
that you **don't** have control over,
problems that are *not caused by you* and
ones you have no control in solving, such as
divorce,
alcohol or drug abuse by others,
physical or verbal abuse

you need to leave them at the doorstep, keep them
separate from you personal life,
and then move on.

If you don't,
they will effect just about every thing you do.

If you don't believe it now, you'll believe it
when you see it.

You can bet the ranch that
many of the people in treatment centers
or in jails
have carried guilt with them for years from
problems caused by others.

This guilt most likely caused frustration, depression
or anger which in turn
caused their drug problem, alcohol problem,
anger problem or whatever problem
that got them in trouble.

If you constantly blame yourself
for other people's problems,
you need to step back and take a good hard look
at what's going on in your life.

Let me show you how
you can go about doing this.

First,
grab a piece of paper and a pen.

Next,
think about all the things that are bothering you
right now
and write them down on the paper.
No matter what they are or how small you think
they may be,
if it bothers you, write it down.

Problems with your girl or boyfriend,
trouble in school, problems at home
—whatever they are—
write them down.

Once you've done that, look over each
of the problems one by one.
If the problem is **yours**
and you have total control over solving it,
put a "**C**" next to it.

If, however, it's a problem that
someone else in your family has and
you don't have any control in solving,
things like alcohol or drug abuse, verbal or physical
abuse, divorce, etc.,
put a "**NC**" next to it.

When you're done, look at the **C**'s on the list. These **Control Problems** are the problems you need to take responsibility for and make right. They are your problems and it is you who must deal with them.

No big thing.

For the **NC**'s, the ones that are not your problems and ones you have **NO CONTROL** over, think about what your options are. I mean, what can you do about them since you have no control in getting them solved? You can't just say, *"well, I'll just forget the feelings I have about what happened to me and get on with my life."* These issues weigh heavy on your mind and are not things you can easily dismiss.

So, what do you do?

I have a suggestion for you.

READ IT VERY CAREFULLY...

THE SITUATION AND THE PERPETRATOR

HAVE NOW BECOME THE MOTIVATOR

The **situation** you were in that has caused you so much guilt, pain, anger and frustration,

and the **person or persons** who were responsible for this situation, have now become your **motivator**.

In other words, you do what **thousands** of young people in your situation have done. You take the anger, frustration and guilt you have from the situation you were in and **make it work for you**.

How? By switching these emotions away from being **a depressing burden** to you, to being tools used to help **motivate** you in achieving your goals in life.

Let me give you a quick **true example**:

Richard was a young boy living in New York City when his father walked out on the family leaving them with nothing. Total poverty. Richard became extremely frustrated and angry thinking he had something to do with it. For years this frustration, anger and the depression that went along with it grew. When Richard was in 7th grade, his anger came to a head when he got mad at a teacher and throw a chair at him. Richard was suspended. A few days later, the principal asked me if I would take him in my program; a program for New York kids that teaches, among other things, about switching anger and frustration from off "your" back and onto "your" goals in life. Gradually he worked on this teaching and more and more worked hard at not allowing himself to switch the anger he had back onto himself. *"I'm gonna make it in school and do something with my life for a change. I'm gonna show dad and everyone else that I AM somebody. Ain't NOTHING gonna stop me."* Richard became focused on keeping the anger off of himself and on to what he had to do to make it in school. To make a long story short, Richard graduated on the honor roll. He now works in Washington DC at the intelligence department of the **United States Navy**.

The **SITUATION** (his father walking out) and the **PER-PETRATOR** (his father) have become the **MOTIVATOR** for his success.

Richard wins in more ways than one.

You say you have no goals in life?

Yeah you do. You, like everyone else, want to "be somebody;" have a decent life; good friends, a nice house, a good job, maybe be married and have a nice family. When you as a kid were asked what you wanted to be when you grew up, you didn't say things like, *"I want to be a bum,"* or **"I want to spend the rest of my life in prison."** Instead you talked about positive things for yourself.

By switching the emotions you feel from the **situation** you were in onto the goals you set for yourself and allow them to be the **motivation** to succeed, you, like Richard, win in more ways than one:

FIRST: You overcome the bad feelings you have because you're not using them to beat yourself up anymore, but rather as a tool to be successful in life. **Different focus, different outcome.**

SECOND: You defeat the p**erpetrator** by taking what he/she has done to you and using the anger caused by it to **motivate you**.

In other words the **perpetrator** has **not** defeated you but rather has **motivated** you.

YOU WIN!

THIRD: You increase the chances of reaching your goals in life and being successful at what you do.

Like I said, there are **thousands** of young people who have **switched** their emotions from being on their back to putting them onto the goals they set for themselves in life. I'm sure you have heard of such people.

FINAL THOUGHT

From movie stars to business people; from athletes to high school students, people have come to realize that when you take the emotions of

"WHAT WAS,"

and apply them to

"WHAT COULD BE,"

YOU WIN.

And the more you **stay focused**, keeping that "switch" on motivating yourself and not allowing it to "click back" to **bring yourself down**, the better you are going to feel about yourself in the end.

So always remember...

THE SITUATION AND THE PERPETRATOR

HAVE NOW BECOME THE MOTIVATOR

Before you set out to achieve a certain goal in your life, ask yourself this question:

"How bad do I really want it?"

If the answer is not all that bad, then I would forget about reaching that goal because chances are really good, you won't.

F A C T   S E V E N

Make no mistake about it:
DESIRE IS THE KEY TO SUCCESS
in just about any goal you set for yourself
in life.

Simply put, DESIRE is how bad
you **really** want something.

Not how bad you *think* you want something,
but how bad you **actually** want it.

The amount of DESIRE you have
in going after your goal will most likely determine
whether you accomplish it or not.

Why is this so?

Because when you're motivated by DESIRE,
when you're "in that zone,"
when you want something **really bad**,
you're going to do whatever it takes to get it.

To put it another way...

Other than breaking the law, hurting yourself
or
hurting other people,

DESIRE IS

"doing what you gotta do to get to where
you wanna get."

That's exactly what Tyrone Bogues did.
He "did what he had to do to get to where he got."

In my opinion, Tryone is the ultimate example of
what it means to have DESIRE.

In the dictionary next to the word
"desire"
there should be a picture of Tyrone.

It was a real tough obstacle to overcome.

No, it wasn't the fact that he grew up in poverty or that his father was arrested for robbery when he was twelve. There was something else Tyrone had to overcome if he ever wanted to fulfill his dream of becoming a basketball player. Something that seemed to bother everyone else much more than it did him.

But Tyrone never listened to what other people had to say anyway. He wanted to play basketball and so he did. He went out for his team and not only started all four years, but guided Dunbar High School to a state championship and through two straight undefeated seasons.

"All right," people said at this point. "High school is fine. But with your handicap, ain't no way you're playing college ball."

Wrong again.

They underestimated the DESIRE this kid had to play the game. Tyrone wanted it and wanted it BAD. Nothing, not even his handicap, was going to stop him.

After he graduated from high school, Tryone attended Wake Forest college. He played basketball all 4 years averaging 11.3 points, 8.4 assists and 3.1 steals a game.

Not bad for a kid with a handicap such as he had.

Then Tryone stated talking about going into the NBA. "Paaa leeese," people would say jokingly. "Ain't no way." People laughed and thought nothing of it. As far as they were concerned, the kid should be happy that he did as well as he did in college. But the NBA? FORGET ABOUT IT!

But once again Tryone believed in what HE could do and not what other people thought he could do. He wanted to play ball and wanted it bad. If only he could get an opportunity to show what he could do. If only the NBA would look past his handicap and give him a chance.

To the amazement to others, Tyrone got the opportunity he hoped for. The Washington Bullets took a chance on him and drafted him in the 13th round. He finally got his "moment in the sun." But could he prove himself? Was his handicap too much for him to overcome? Would DESIRE win out over LOGIC or would LOGIC prevail?

To make a long story short, DESIRE did win over LOGIC. Not only did he play in the NBA (the Charlotte Hornets), but he was the teams leader in time played, assists, steals, turnovers and has a career average of 11.2 point a game. What's more amazing is that this man played in the NBA for **11 years** in spite of the fact that he was born with the handicap of being only **5' 3" tall**, standing just below the chest or at best chest level of most NBA players. The shortest man to ever play in the NBA with the likes of Jordan and all the other greats.

Tryone "Muggsy" Bogues is a great example of how the DESIRE to want to succeed will win out over the logic to quit if a person is willing to work hard enough to achieve his or her goals.

If there was only one poster hanging on the wall in my room to motivate me in WHATEVER goal I wanted to succeed in, it would be that of "Muggsy" Bogues, the little kid who could.

Fact is,

take any great athlete, business person, musician, actor or anyone who is successful in what they do and the bottom line is always the same:

They wanted it bad enough to do whatever it took to achieve their goal.

FINAL THOUGHT

I have two questions for you

First,
what goals are you trying to achieve for yourself?

Second,
when you get knocked down in the process
of trying to reach your goals,
how many times will it take to keep you down?

FACT EIGHT

There are a number of reasons why a person becomes depressed.

For teenagers, however,

four reasons
stand out most of all:

The first has to do with a chemical imbalance in
the brain.

This is not uncommon.

Things like
a serious change in
sleeping habits,
constant sadness
or
crying for no reason

could all be signs of depression caused by a
chemical imbalance in the brain.

If you feel you suffer from depression,
one of the first things you want to do
is get a check-up from the doctor.

He or she will be able to determine if the
depression you have is due to a
medical problem.

If so, there is medication that can help.

In fact,
statistics show that ninety percent of the people who
are on medication because of depression respond
favorably.

The second reason for depression has to do with what is called the

BLAME GAME.

The blame game happens when people blame themselves for everything that goes wrong in their family no matter how obvious it is that *they had nothing to do with it.*

The bottom line to the BLAME GAME is simple:

Anytime you blame yourself for family problems you have no control over, things such as divorce, abuse, alcohol, drugs, etc.,

the problem automatically becomes yours as well.

Carrying this unnecessary burden on your back can't help but cause you to be depressed.

One, two, three,
A, B, C,
it can't be any easier that that.

Read more about this important reason for depression in **Fact #6**.

~

The next major cause for depression
has to do with something called

Murphy's Law Plus.

You've heard of Murphy's Law, haven't you?

Murphy's Law states that if anything can
go wrong in life, it probably will.

Murphy's Law *Plus* takes this saying
one step further:

It states that even if things go good in life,
something will come along to mess it up anyway,
so what's the use of feeling good about it?

So,

When things go bad in life,
the person is going to feel bad.

When things go good in life,
the person is still going to feel bad.

How can a person *not* be depressed with thinking
like this?

People who suffer from Murphy's Law Plus
must understand that
good things come along in life
more often than not.

When they do, they should be exploited
for all it's worth.

To help you better understand this,
consider the following story...

Driving home from work one day, I stopped to watch a local Little League baseball game. As I sat down behind the bench on the first-base line, I asked one of the boys what the score was.

"We're behind, 14 to nothing," he answered, smiling.

"Really," I said, "I have to say you don't look very discouraged."

"Discouraged?" the boy asked with a puzzled look. "Why should we be discouraged?

"We haven't been up to bat yet."

The point of this story is simple.

No matter how bad things seem to be in life,
you're always going to get your turn at bat
when it comes to feeling good about something.

The question is,
will you choose to take advantage of it
or
will you just
stand at the plate and not swing at the ball
because you figure,

*"What's the use? The ball game is going to
eventually end anyway,
so why have fun playing it now?"*

~

To deal with MURPHY'S LAW PLUS, you first
need to understand that the reason you feel life is so
depressing has nothing to do with MURPHY'S LAW,

but rather how you perceive life based first on
how you feel about yourself as a person.

The better you feel about yourself as a person, the
better life will seem to be for you.

To understand this better, go to **Fact #10**.

The last reason for depression has to do
with a person's inability to connect
with other people.

These could very well be people who have many
friends and are liked by others,
but still feel an inadequacy about themselves.

To them, it just seems as though
everyone else
is better than they are.

To get a real good understanding of why
this kind of depression is baseless,
you'd be wise to read the story

**THE SEARCH FOR SHELBY
starting on page 181.**

The story will help you understand where
your value really lies and why depression
such as this is *unrealistic*.

I wouldn't be able to explain it any better.

DEALING WITH DEPRESSION

No matter what the cause of depression
may be,
one this is for sure:

Things do get better in life if you work hard
to solve the problems that may be causing
the depression...

and stick around to see
what the results will be.

The most obvious way to do this
is to get some help.

Sure,
I know what you're thinking...

"If I get some help,
people are going to know I have problems.
...Besides,
getting help is a sign of weakness."

(Like **not** getting help when you're hurting is a
sign of strength?)

Fact is, getting help for your problems
is a sign of

self respect,

not weakness.

That's because when you get help for what's
bothering you,
things in life do get better.

And, anytime you want things
to get better for yourself,
there's always an element of
self respect
involved.

Unfortunately, not everyone believes this.

One can certainly understand why.

When you're depressed and everything
seems to be caving in on you
all at once,

you're not focused on life getting
better for you,
you're focused on how bad life is right now.

I'm sure this was the way Eleanor Wilson felt.

Although it is quite obvious that a vast
majority of teenagers handle their depression
much differently than Eleanor did,
this true story is still a good example
of how some people
let ***depression*** rule over ***logic***.

Eleanor Wilson was a struggling actress back in the 1940's who wanted nothing more than to be a movie star.

She auditioned for every part that came her way, no matter how small it was. She did get some bit parts here and there, but never landed the role that would put her name up in lights.

The lack of progress in her career made her frustrated, angry and finally seriously depressed. When drinking and drugs didn't help, she decided to end it all.

For her, life was as good as it was going to get.

One day, Eleanor trudged up to the top floor of a 40 story building in New York City, walked out onto the roof and jumped off—falling to her death.

Eleanor died believing that her depression, and what caused it, would last forever.

Unfortunately for her, she was wrong.

Two days later, her agent received a phone call from a huge movie production company. The studio wanted Eleanor to take the lead role in what would have been a major motion picture.

When the agent received the script, he was shocked at what he read.

You see, the role Eleanor would have played was that of a woman who was so depressed about her life that she climbed to the top of a building in New York City, walked onto the roof and jumped off the edge, falling to her death.

There is no doubt that if Eleanor had sought the help she needed to work on the problems that caused her depression, she would have been the star she always wanted to be.

Unfortunately, Eleanor played out her role too soon.

FINAL THOUGHT

To review, there are four main reasons for depression. If you suffer from depression, it would be wise to discuss these ideas with someone who can help.

1. Chemical imbalance
2. The BLAME GAME
3. Murphy's Law Plus
4. An inability to connect with other people.

The bottom line to depression is simple:

Think more of yourself in terms of getting the help you need,

than you do of what others may think of you for doing so.

--Get to a doctor for a check up. (Pg. 136)
--Find someone you can trust to talk to (Pg. 143)
--Never, NEVER, take the blame for problems that have absolutely nothing to do with you. (Pg. 111)
--Learn the difference between problems you have control over and problems you don't have control over. (Pg. 119)

As bad as a situation may seem to you, things DO get better in life if you make the effort to get the help you need.

" *What, are you nuts?*
Not me!
I'd rather have
no friends
for doing the right thing,
than hang out with
a hundred people
who think I'm cool
for doing something
stupid."

FACT NINE

This was the response from
one teenager to another
when the teenager said the following:

"I know the people I hang out with don't really like me.

"In fact, the only time they hang out with me is when I smoke weed with them.

"Every other time it's like they don't even know me.

"But I still hand out with them anyway."

"Why do you do that?" the other teenager asked.

"Because I'd rather hang out with people who don't like me and smoke a little weed with them...

"...than not hang out with anyone at all."

The boy's response makes up FACT #9 on
page 149,

and I agree.

I agree because I know for a *fact*
that if a person respects him or herself first,
other people will respect that person in return.

No one needs to do **ANYTHING**,
much less disrespect themselves,
to get people to like them.

That's just the way it is.

Read **THE SEARCH FOR SHELBY** story
starting on page 181 to see
why it is

the way it is.

<u>FINAL THOUGHT</u>

There is an old saying that summarizes this
chapter really well.

It goes like this:

*There's no bigger fool than
a person
who is influenced by a fool.*

Unfortunately, too many teenagers
find this out
the hard way.

Hopefully, you're smart enough not to be
one of them.

**F
A
C
T**

*There are two types of
people
who will hang out
with you...*

**T
E
N**

...those who hang out with you because
they respect you as a person

and

those who hang out with you because
they're impressed with the
negative image
you've created for yourself.

For those people who hang out with you
because they respect you as a person,
you have what are called

"*Cover Your Back Friends.*"

These are people who respect *you for who you are*
and
who will stick with you through
the good times as well as the bad.

They are the kinds of friends everyone
would like to have.

For those people who hang out with you because
they're impressed with the *negative image*
you've created for yourself,
keep in mind
that there's a price to be paid.

The *negative image* you create for yourself
becomes the image people know you by.

The *negative image* people
know you by
becomes the *negative image*
you must maintain
in order to keep the so-called friends
who hang out with you.

Keeping these so-called friends will depend on
how long you keep up the *negative image*.

Herein lies the problem.

Sooner or later the *negative image*
you've created for yourself is going
to fade away
and the reality of who
you really are as a person
will be exposed.

Either people will get tired of the image
you've created
or
it will end up getting
you into trouble somehow.

Jails and drug rehab centers are full of people
whose negative *image*
has simply gotten them in trouble.

When this happens to you,
what will be your next move?

Will the same insecurity which
created the *negative image*
in the first place
cause you to create a new one?

Maybe even a much tougher one?

Or,
will you finally realize that **respect** is
not something you get for bad behavior,
but rather something **earned** for
just being **who you are?**

For all of those whose image
has "broken" and would like to find ways of
"getting it fixed,"
here's a couple of suggestions for you.

First, you must develop what is called a
Sense of Identity.

In other words,
you need to know who you are and what it is about
you that would make other people want
to hang out with you.

I don't want to sound
like "Joe Psychiatrist" or anything...
but let's face it, the reason you saw a need to
change your image in the first place
is because you're not happy with
the natural identity you already have.

The next section can help you to discover what
makes you...*you*.

The next thing you need to do is read
THE SEARCH FOR SHELBY
starting on page 181.

In it you will understand why all the time
and effort you use to get people to like you
is time and effort that is wasted.

HOW TO FIND YOUR IDENTITY

To discover what it is that makes people want
to hang out with you,
you must first determine what makes you
such a valuable person.

To understand this, you need to
do away with the notion

that your looks
or
the things you do

has anything to do with who you are
as a person.

This is a very common mistake
too many teenagers make.

They base their values on their looks or on the
things they do and actually believe that this
determines how many friends they're
going to have.

If you stop and think about it, you'll see
how ridiculous this really is.

If you base your value on what you do
or how you look

then it would be safe to say that people who
don't "look right" or who "can't do anything"
because they're either
mentally or physically handicapped,
are people who have absolutely no value
to anyone.

That's crazy.
Only a shallow person would believe this.

Let me give you an example of what I mean...

A few years back, there was a situation that happened to a 6 year old boy named David. You may have seen or heard about it on the news.

His parents were going through a bitter divorce and there was no way his father would let David live with his mother. Coming up with a plan he thought would solve the problem, David's dad took his son to a motel. It was late. David was tired and went right to bed after he got into the room. His father sat in a chair next to him and waited.

When David was fast asleep, his father slowly rose from the chair, went out to the car, opened the trunk and pulled out a can of kerosene.

When he went back into the room, he checked one more time to make sure that David was sound asleep. He was.

His father then opened the can, sprinkled the kerosene around his little boy on the bed and lit a match. "If I can't have you in this divorce," he thought to himself, "neither will your mother."

He then threw the lit match on the bed, waited to make sure the bed caught fire and then walked out the door.

The tiny flame burst into a blaze. The bedspread
caught on fire. David's clothes caught on fire.
David was on fire.

He rolled to the floor in fear as he tried to put out
the flames that engulfed his body.

Firefighters eventually came and quickly wrapped
blankets around the boy trying to smother the flames.

David survived.

However, he was in bad shape. Most of his body was
badly burned. His fingers were nothing but numbs
and what was left of his hair looked like little strands
of thread. His face was so badly burned, there was
no way you could even recognize him. In addition,
David had to wear a special mask on his face
to help graft together the burnt skin.

Everything that **society says** makes a person valuable
- things like what a person **DOES** or how a person
LOOKS - was taken from David. He had no LOOKS
to speak of because of the mask and the burns under-
neath, and certainly was in no shape do DO anything.

If you buy into this concept that the things you **DO**
or the way you **LOOK** give a person value, then
it would be safe to say that David had absolutely **no
value** to anyone as a person. David would be useless.
But like I said earlier, only a shallow person would
believe this.

This was made clear a few years later when David's mom called a news conference to let the public know how her son was doing.

The televised news conference was held in a large room where a crowd of reporters gathered to hear what David had to say. A long table was set up in front of the room and a dozen or so microphones were grouped together facing a chair where David was to sit.

In time, David slowly made his way in from the right side of the room. He wore gray sweatpants, a gray sweatshirt, a White Sox baseball hat and he still wore the mask on his face to protect his skin. He painfully walked toward the empty chair aided by a nurse on one arm and his mother on the other.

When David got to the empty chair, he carefully sat down. In the process, you could see his eyes squint with pain between the brim of his hat and the mask on his face. Sitting behind all those microphones, the only thing visible on David was his hat.

After he was seated, the reporters began to ask him questions. "How are you doing, David?"

"How do you feel, David?"

"What are you going to do now, David?"

In answering the questions, I was impressed with the boy's composure. I mean, this kid was *cool*. He could have easily let his anger and hatred for what his father did do all the talking for him, but he didn't let that happen.

Instead, David was simply David. He was confident; he was strong; he had a good sense of humor, and he communicated in such a way that made viewers from all around the country fall in love with him.

The point of this true story is simple:

what defined who this little boy *really* was
didn't have anything to do
with what he did or how he looked.

I hope this is true with you as well.

If it isn't,
don't expect the people *you hang out with*,
to be *hanging out with you* for very long.

If you get what I mean.

~

So then, what was it?

What did David have that made so many people
like and respect him?

What is it you have that would make others want
to hang out with you?

To answer this question,
think of someone you really admire.
Someone you really look up to.
Maybe someone you consider your hero.

What draws you to this person?
What is it about this person you like?

If we are talking about respect for
who the person is and *not* for what
he or she *does*
or how this person *looks*,
chances are you admire the person because
the person is sure of who he or she is.

The person has certain characteristics
that come across with confidence and with
an air of self respect in them.

For example,
the person may be be someone who is
"cool under pressure," like David,
or is independent and doesn't need others to make
decisions for him or her.

He or she may be a person
with a good sense of humor and you're impressed
with the ease in which he or she delivers
that humor.

There are hundreds of characteristic traits
that may define who a person really is.

Unlike the negative image a person may put up to try
to impress people, traits like these
are life-long qualities *that won't fade in time*.

They are the things that truly define who you are
as a person and traits that make the kind of friends
who will stick around.

It is the "rock" I talked about on page 14.

~

So, back to my original question...

What is it that other people respect about you?

What is it about you that would make other people
want to hang out with you?

Don't know? Maybe the next few pages
can help you find out.

On them is a list of the more common characteristic
traits people have that draw people to one another.
See if you have any that stand out.

Keep in mind that these are only a few of the characteristics people possess.

You may have others.

You're a person who...

❑　　　*has a good sense of humor.* You can make people laugh.

❑　　　*has compassion for other people*, and you're not afraid to show it toward anyone.

❑　　　*is cool under pressure.* You take things in stride no matter how serious the situation may be.

❑　　　*isn't afraid to stand up for what is right* no matter what others may think and no matter what the consequences may be.

❑　　　*is easygoing, laid back.* People can mess around with you and you don't take it personally.

❑　　　*is loyal.* You're there for friends or relatives when they really need you.

❑　　　*never quits.* You're a tough person. No matter how many time you get "knocked down" in life by family problems, personal problems or problems with friends you keep "getting up."

❑   *treats others with respect.* You're not the kind of person who puts people down or talks about them behind their backs.

❑   *is independent.* You're not led around by your friends; you'd rather think for yourself. You're also a person who can get along fine by just hanging out with yourself. You have the kind of confidence others see and admire.

❑   *has strong convictions.* Whether it be religion, values, social issues or whatever—you stick to your views no matter what other people think.

❑   *has good leadership skills.* When things get tough, people look to you for leadership. You're the kind of person people can turn to for answers in tough situations. You think for yourself and don't allow others to influence your decisions.

Like I said, these are just a few of the things that could make up who you are as a person. Are there others? There always are. If so, what are they?

Give it some thought.

If you want a more objective opinion of the kind
of person you really are,
and
possibly a more **honest one**,

give the list of Characteristic Traits on pages
170 & 171 to a friend,
or a girlfriend or boyfriend
and ask him or her to check off what
it is about you
that makes them want to hang out with you.

Chances are good
that you're probably going to be surprised at
the traits they check off.

After all,
what you **think** you act like
and how other people **really see** you as a person
are usually two different things.

If you're dating, giving this list to your
girl/boy friend is a great way
to find out what he or she
REALLY
likes about you.

No matter what they check off, the truth will always
be the same.

That is, if more people
worked as hard at being *respected* as they do at
trying to be *popular*, they would save themselves
a whole lot of problems when it comes to attracting
the kind of people they want to
hang out with.

The reason for this is simple:

When you be who you are,
***some people will** be attracted*
to your kind of personality,
some won't
*and **most won't care** one way or the other.*

That's just the way it is.

However, the people you do attract from being who
you are are people who hang out with you
because they like and respect you first as a person
and not because of some superficial thing
you may have done to get their attentions.

Simply put...

IF IT COMES FROM WITHIN,
YOU KNOW IT'S RIGHT.

This differs from those who try to be *popular*
by being superficial and because they worry about
EVERYBODY liking them,
they do things not based on *who they are*
but rather based on what
they think *other people want to see*.

A good example of this could be seen
at high school parties where there's drinking
or drugs being used.

Question:

Are the people who are drinking alcohol or taking
drugs doing it to be *respected* or to be *popular*?

I think we both know the answer to that.

In that lies the problem as to why some people
struggle to be *truly* accepted by others.

FINAL THOUGHT

Constantly seeking the approval of other people by the things you **do** or the way you **look** only serves to justify your own self worth and is only a temporary fix in helping you to feel that you have value to other people. It only lasts as long as the next person you try to impress.

Understand the following and
save yourself a lot of pain in your life:

There is only one person you need to seek the approval from. When you get the approval from that one person, you will not see a need to seek it from everyone else. To find out who that person is, read ***THE SEARCH FOR SHELBY*** on page **181**.

Putting it another way:
you don't pick and choose your personality.
You don't say things like...
"I'm going to act like this to this person"
or
"I'm going act like this to that person."

This makes no sense!

You don't pick and choose your personality,
you **EXPLOIT IT**.
You take the things that **define who you are**
and make them work **FOR YOU**.

Time for a reality check...

Before you read the following story,
let me warn you
that it is a strange one.

It's the kind of story you will understand,
but yet,
you won't understand it.

As the author,
I certainly understand it,
but I too can't figure out how
the man made it happen.

You'll know what I'm talking about
once you read it.

One thing about this story, however,
is very clear:
the message being conveyed to you.

Once you figure out what it is,

ask yourself if it is the kind of thing
you practice in your own life.

If not, maybe it's time you did.

One thing is for sure:
EVERYONE,

from the big "bad" gang member to
the most timid student,

EVERYONE
searches for the Town of Shelby
in his or her life.

NO ONE is exempt,

NO ONE.

The only difference between those who find it and
those who don't lies in the way
one goes about looking.

(See FACT #10.)

THE SEARCH FOR SHELBY

The back of the school bus was Casey's favorite place to sit... not just the back, but the last seat, next to the window. That was Casey's seat and everybody knew it.

It wasn't that this particular seat was any safer or more comfortable than the others. In fact, "comfortable" would be the last word Casey would use to describe it.

It was just that the corner seat was a place for Casey to get away from everyone. It was a place for her to hide.

Casey was a loner, an outsider. She kept pretty much to herself. She bothered no one, and no one really paid much attention to her. Usually she would rest her head against the window and fall asleep until she got to school.

Casey's parents had divorced about two years earlier and this weighed heavy on her mind. She blamed herself for the divorce. She didn't exactly know why, but she must've had something to do with it.

Ever since the divorce, Casey had turned within herself and shut everyone else out of her life.

As much as she wanted friends, as much as she wanted people to like her, she had lost all confidence in who she was and in her ability to have any friends.

"Dad left the family so he must not care about me," she figured, "and I'm sure no one else does either. So, everybody, just leave me alone."

Those were hard times for Casey. If it wasn't for Pop being there when she needed him, no telling what would've happened.

"Pop" was her bus driver's nickname. Nobody really knew what his real name was. In fact, every once in a while, Casey would try to get him to tell her.

But he never would.

Instead, he'd always say the same thing to Casey, "When I'm ready to tell someone, you'll be the first to know."

As much as Casey wondered about Pop's real name, Pop wondered why Casey was always alone. It just didn't make any sense to him.

This was a great kid with a great personality, yet the only person who didn't seem to believe it was Casey herself.

From time to time Pop would talk to her about this, but nothing ever seemed to come of it.

In fact, their conversation became routine, boring, almost predictable. Casey would always talk about how insecure she was around other people, how everybody just seemed better than she was and how trying to make friends was just a waste of time.

"Why should I waste my time trying to get people to like me when I know it's not gonna happen?" she would tell Pop. Pop, on the other hand, was no less predictable in his response.

He would patiently listen to Casey and then would always tell her the same thing; it was always the same thing,

"Oftentimes Casey,
the things we search for most in life,
things like friendship and respect, are things
that have been with us all along.
My hope is that you will one day
understand this."

"What the heck is he talking about?" Casey would always ask herself..

Pop's response to Casey was so predictable that it got to a point where Casey would lip-sync the words as Pop was saying them.

Morning after morning, Casey trudged back to her seat, dropped her backpack on the seat next to her, plopped into her place, rested her head against the window, and fell asleep. It became routine for her.

But as Casey was about to find out, routines sometimes have a way of changing. And this routine was about to change in a most unusual way. It happened on a boring Monday, of all days.

Casey headed for her seat as usual, dropped her backpack on the seat next to her, plopped into her place, rested her head against the window, and immediately dozed off. When the old bus arrived at school, the squeaking of brakes woke Casey up as it did every morning.

She stretched a bit and glanced past the window as she opened her eyes and reached for her backpack. When she turned to look out the window again, she saw something peculiar.

A small group of kids her age were waving at her and motioning her to come off the bus.

Casey rubbed her eyes to get a better look.

"Who are those people?" she said as she quickly turned away in shyness. "Why are they waving at me?"

Casey sneaked another look. Maybe they'd be gone. Maybe they were waving at somebody else. But they weren't.

Casey pointed to herself as if to say, "Me? You want me?"

The group nodded in agreement.

Casey grabbed her backpack, slowly got up from her seat and reluctantly walked to the front of the empty bus. "I don't know them," she kept saying to herself. "Why do they want me? I don't know those kids."

When she came to the bus steps, she stopped and turned toward the driver's seat. There was Pop. "Who are those people, Pop?" Casey asked. Pop smiled at her, but he said nothing. Casey turned back to the kids outside the open bus door.

"You want me?" she asked.

The kids again motioned for her to come with them.

"Come on, Casey," one called. "Come with us."

Casey cautiously started down the steps.

A boy with red hair and a nice smile did most of the talking. "Hi, Casey! How ya doing?" he said. "Good to see you again."

Everyone in the group agreed.

"Good to see me again?" Casey asked with a confused look on her face. "Who are you? How do you know my name? I don't know any of you. Where am I?"

"Don't you know?" the red-haired boy asked. "You're in Shelby. You know where Shelby is. You've been in Shelby all your life. What's wrong with you?

"What a dumb question. We're your friends. Don't you remember anything?"

Casey still looked confused.

"What the heck are they talking about?" she asked herself. "What's going on here? My friends? Been in Shelby all my life?"

"Come on," a girl from the group said, interrupting Casey's thoughts, "we're going to get something to eat, and we want you to come with us, Casey. Come on."

Again, everyone in the group agreed.

Casey slowly shook her head back and forth. "No," she said, "I... I can't go with you. I don't know who you are. You've got the wrong person. You don't know me, so you can't like me. Nobody likes me."

Now it was the group's turn to look confused.

Casey paused again, then said, "I have to get back on the bus. I'll be late for school. I've got to go."

"Wait!" said the red-haired boy. "You know us. You must not remember. Come with us, Casey. You won't be late. We really want you to come."

"No," Casey said as she backed up the steps. "You don't know me. Nobody knows me. I... I've got to go."

Confused, Casey quickly walked up the steps to the back of the bus and then huddled in her usual seat. Shortly after, a deep voice interrupted Casey's sleep. This time it wasn't the people at the bottom of the steps. It was Pop.

"Come on," he said. "Come on, Casey, wake up. You're going to be late for school if you don't get going."

Casey slowly opened her eyes, looked at Pop, then quickly turned to look out the window.

"Pop!" she said. "Where did those kids go? Who are they?"

"You all right, Casey?" he asked. "You better get going. It's 8:15."

Casey paused a moment. Reality slowly set in as she began to realize that she must have been dreaming. "8:15? Did you say 8:15, Pop? I'm gonna be late!" She quickly grabbed her backpack, paused one more time to look out the window and then ran off the bus.

All day long at school, Casey thought about that morning and how real it all seemed to be. She could hardly think of anything else.

On the one hand, she knew it was probably just some silly dream. But on the other hand, her feeling of having been wanted and accepted by those people was so strong, so real. She had never felt like that before.

It was strange, but it was a good feeling to have.

By day's end, though, a sad, lonely feeling had crept deep into Casey's soul. She knew she could never have friends who liked her that much. How she wished the people from Shelby had been more than just a dream.

~

The next morning, Casey hurried to her usual seat on the bus. "I wonder if I could," she thought as she sat down. "I wonder if I could go back to that town."

Before she knew it, she was asleep, her head resting against the cold window.

Shortly after the bus stopped, Casey woke up and looked out the window. Sure enough, there were all her "friends" motioning to her to get off the bus.

This time she didn't hesitate. Casey raced to the front of the empty bus and stopped only long enough to glance at the driver's seat. There was Pop.

Once again, he just smiled.

Casey turned back toward the door and slowly walked down the steps to greet her "friends."

"Come on, Casey! Come with us today," the boy with the red hair said.

"Yeah, Casey, come with us. We want you to be with us," said another one of the kids.

"Where are we going?" Casey asked.

"We're gonna get something to eat, then walk around Shelby. We're just gonna mess around and have some fun."

Though she still didn't understand, Casey wasn't about to resist this time. "Let's do it," she said, and all were off to Shelby.

Everyone Casey met as she and her friends walked down the quiet, tree-lined streets of Shelby seemed to know her.

Everyone.

It was the most incredible, most gratifying, most beautiful experience she had ever had in her life.

No matter where she went, whether it was to someone's house, or to the mall, or just hanging out at the corner store, Casey was overwhelmed by the way everyone treated her and by the respect and warmth they showed her.

It was so easy to be in Shelby, to just be herself and to laugh again.

It had been a long time since she felt like this. It reminded her of those Christmas days when her dad was home and her family was all together and happy.

It was exactly what she had been searching for ever since her mom and dad divorced.

She had only one regret: that she had to wake up and leave the town of Shelby at the end of the day.

Each school day now, Casey hurried to her usual seat on the bus in anticipation of spending time with her friends in Shelby.

Each day, her friends would be there to greet her. When Casey saw them, she'd rush to the front of the bus, glance at Pop, then join her friends.

But one day before she left the bus, she gave Pop a long look. She just had to ask:

"Pop, I... I don't understand what's going on here. These people – why do they like me so much? I didn't do anything to get them to like me."

Pop smiled his usual "Pop" smile, then he answered Casey:

"Oftentimes, the things we search for most in life..."

Before Pop could finish, Casey jumped in, "Yeah, yeah I know,

'are things that have been with us all along.' "

Casey smiled and then turned to step off the bus, glancing back at Pop one more time. "This is crazy," she thought, shaking her head, "This is nuts."

There was no doubt Casey enjoyed her friends' company, and they enjoyed hers. She had never received this kind of attention and affection from anyone in her life.

But the same questions kept nagging her, "What's going on here? Why do these people like me?" Casey was determined to get some answers. If Pop couldn't give them to her, maybe her friends could.

One day, while having lunch at the mall with her friends, she decided to give it a try.

Sitting across from her in the booth was the red-haired boy. Both were waiting for the rest of the group to get their food.

Casey spoke up, "Hey, umm, maybe you can help me out," she said to the red-haired boy as she nervously moved things around on her tray. "I, ahhh, I just can't understand something. I don't understand what's going on here.

"What am I doing here? Why does everybody like me? I don't understand. I'm no great athlete or nothing. I'm certainly not the best-looking person in the world, that's for sure. What's going on here?"

The red-haired boy unwrapped his burger, smoothed out the paper, then looked up at Casey to answer her. "You don't have to do nothing for us. We just like you, that's all. We just like you.

"Why do you think you have to do something to get us to like you?" There was a pause while the boy took a small bite out of his burger.

Shortly after, he spoke up again. This time he stared straight into Casey's eyes. "Don't you get it, Casey?" he told her. "All these things happening to you—they are all things Shelby's been trying to tell you. They are all things Shelby has been trying to tell you for a long time. This is what Shelby is really all about."

Casey slowly leaned back in her booth. "Shelby's been trying to tell me this for a long time?" she whispered to herself, "He's worse than Pop."

Casey may not have understood what was going on, but she did know she wanted to be in Shelby.

There, the sun was always shining, and every day was as warm as the people she was with. She enjoyed her friends' company, and—surprisingly, Casey thought—they enjoyed hers.

She had rarely gotten this kind of attention and affection from anyone in her life.

Gradually Casey's thoughts of worthlessness were worn down by her feelings of confidence and happiness. She wished she could stay in Shelby forever. But that was not to be.

That's because the day Casey feared most was about to arrive.

On this day, Casey rushed to her corner seat as usual, tossed her backpack next to her, and fell asleep as she always did.

When the squeaking of the brakes woke her up, she looked out the window and noticed that her friends weren't waiting for her.

Casey frantically looked out the window. "What happened?" she asked herself. "Where are they? Where are my friends?"

Casey grew anxious.

She tried to go back to sleep again and again, but to no avail. Every time she woke up, no one was there.

"Casey," Pop called as he looked into the huge rearview mirror. "It's time to go. Come on, you're gonna be late."

Casey didn't answer.

"Casey? You all right? You better get going. You're gonna be late."

Still no answer.

Pop walked to the back of the bus to see what was going on. "Casey, what are you doing?" he asked. "You all right?"

Casey opened her eyes.

"Pop," she asked, "where are those kids?"

"What are you talking about, Casey?" Pop said. "You better get going. I have to get the bus back to the garage, and you have to go to school."

"Pop," she insisted, "you know what I'm talking about. The kids I've been hanging out with—where are they?"

"Casey, you're not making any sense. You just had a dream or something. You better get going or you're gonna be late."

"But Pop..." Casey slowly lowered her eyes in disappointment. She knew Pop was right.

There would be no Shelby today. In fact, there was no Shelby the rest of the week.

As hard as she tried to bring it back, she could not. Maybe... maybe it was just a dream.

Every day, Casey rushed to her seat, dropped her backpack next to her, and fell asleep in hopes of being with her Shelby friends...but nothing.

Shelby would be no more and Casey knew it. The love, attention and affection she had felt in those brief moments of time were now gone.

It had all disappeared.

The school bus stopped in front of Casey's house as it did every Friday afternoon. She got off the bus, but instead of heading for her house, she walked to her favorite "getaway" spot, which was in a small alley behind Buck's grocery store.

There, alone, she leaned her back against the cement wall, dropped her backpack, and slid down the wall to the ground. She pulled her knees up close to her body and rested her arms across them.

"Shelby," she said to herself, "where are you? Where in the heck did you go?"

Casey was deep in thought about Shelby when she was interrupted by the sound of footsteps coming toward her. She lifted her head, trying to focus her eyes through her tears.

As the figure came closer, Casey recognized who it was.

It was Pop.

"Pop!" Casey said, surprised to see him. "What are you doing here?"

"This is a shortcut to my house from the store. What are you doing here?"

Casey rested her chin on her arms, "Just thinking."

Pop pulled an old wooden crate towards him and slowly sat down, placing his small bag of groceries on the ground next to him.

"What are you thinking about?" he asked gently.

Thoughts flew around in Casey's head like a whirlwind, "Should I tell him? Should I tell him about what happened? I really don't want to tell anyone. Maybe he'll think I'm crazy or something. I think I'm crazy or something.

"...But if I can't trust Pop, who can I trust? I just gotta tell someone."

Casey wiggled a bit to get more comfortable. Then, staring at Pop as if to say, "Are you ready for this?" she began to speak.

"Well, this is going to sound crazy to you, Pop, but here goes."

Casey began to tell her story . . .

". . . and when I woke up, I was in this beautiful town with all these really nice people. Everybody in town knew me, Pop, and they were real nice to me—especially the kids. It was like they had known me forever. I never felt so good in all my life. I felt like I was somebody important, somebody special. I felt respected. I didn't even have to try.

"I wish I really had friends like that." Casey paused as she eased back into her original sitting position.

"Then one day I woke up and nothing. No town, no people, no friends, no nothing. Just like it is today—just like it's been forever.

"This may sound silly to you, Pop, but I miss that town. I miss those people really bad. I wish I could go back. I wish I could see them again."

There was a pause as Pop fiddled with his groceries. Then he asked Casey an odd question, "What's the name of this town you were in?"

Casey stared at the ground for a moment in thought, "He wants to know the name of the town? Here I am, telling him all this personal stuff, and he wants to know the name of the town?

"He must think I'm really nuts."

Silence hung in the air between them.

Casey slowly lifted up her head to look at Pop.

"Never mind, Pop," she said. "I talked too much already. Never mind."

Pop said nothing. Instead, he grabbed his bag of groceries and slowly stood up to leave.

Before he got too far, Casey spoke up. "Hey Pop," she said. "see you Monday."

Pop turned, smiled, nodded his head and continued to walk away. As Pop was leaving the alley, an eerie, cold, depressing feeling raced through Casey's body.

She didn't know it at the time, but this depressing chill would soon have merit.

~

Monday morning came too quickly for Casey. She had spent much of the weekend thinking about Shelby and all that had happened.

It was tough to get going, but eventually she was ready for school. Grabbing her backpack, she said goodbye to her mom and headed for the bus.

The bus was unusually late this morning. This was strange because Pop was never late.

When it finally did arrive, it stopped at the curb as the doors swung open.

"Hey, Pop! Where've you been?" Casey said as she started up the steps. "Wait a minute—you're not Pop."

"No," the new bus driver said sadly. "I'm Donna."

"Where's Pop?" Casey asked.

Donna paused before answering.

"He passed away in his sleep this weekend," she said in a soft voice. "I'm sorry."

Casey froze. "Pop? Dead?" she asked in disbelief. "That can't be. I was just talking to him a few days ago. He was fine."

The driver slowly hung her head, saying nothing more about it.

Casey's body was numb. Pop's death cut deeply into her very soul. Ever since she could remember, Pop had always been there for her.

Casey slowly turned and started to trudge to her seat. As she did, the bus driver spoke up.

"Uh, excuse me. You wouldn't happen to be Casey, would you?" she asked.

Casey looked back and nodded as she quickly wiped a tear from her cheek.

"My boss asked me to give you this envelope."

Casey absent-mindedly took the envelope and stuck it in her back pocket before heading to the back of the bus. If there had been a seat on the back bumper, she would've gladly taken it. More than ever, she wanted to be alone.

Casey stared out the window as tears streamed down her face. As fast as the tears came, she'd wipe them away, not wanting anyone to see her cry. She couldn't believe Pop was gone.

Seems like everyone she had ever loved—her father, her friends in Shelby, and now Pop—had disappeared from her life.

This was going to be a long day for Casey and indeed it was. The ride home was even longer.

As Casey stepped off the bus, she again decided to head for her favorite spot in the alley. This time she ran.

When she got there, she threw her backpack on the ground and immediately slid down the wall to sit. She pulled her knees up close to her body, wrapped her arms around her legs, and rested her forehead on her knees.

Tears streamed from her eyes as she began to cry uncontrollably.

"Why did you have to go, Pop?" she thought. "Why did you have to go?"

The alley echoed with the sounds of sadness.

Then suddenly she felt something uncomfortable in her back pocket.

She reached back and pulled out the envelope Donna had given her on the bus.

The letter was short and to the point.

Dear Casey,

Oftentimes the things we search for most in life, things like friendship and respect, are things that have been with us all along.

They come without effort to anyone who believes they possess them. I hope now you believe.

I've been trying to tell you this.

Now you know.

Your friend always,

Shelby

208

"Shelby?" she whispered to herself. "What the heck is going on here?"

Then it hit her.

"Shelby! Could Pop's real name be Shelby?

"It is! Pop's real name is Shelby."

A cold chill slowly crept into her body.

It was then she remembered what the red-haired boy had told her in the mall restaurant,

*"All these things happening to you ...
they are all things Shelby's been
trying to tell you.*

*They are all things Shelby's been trying
to tell you for a long time."*

Casey lifted her eyes in deep thought.

"'Things Shelby's been trying to tell me,'" she whispered. "Could it be? But how? How could he...?"

What Casey was thinking just didn't seem possible.

But it was.

You see, Shelby wasn't about any town. It was more than that...much more. You might say Shelby was Pop's farewell gift to Casey before he died, his way of saying to her,

> *"If you didn't understand me*
> *when I tried to tell you,*
> *maybe you'd understand if I showed you."*

And show her he did.

In a strange, eerie turn of events that could have been taken right from the pages of <u>The Twilight Zone</u>, Shelby the town was really the words of Shelby the man played out for Casey right in front of her eyes.

It was everything Pop (or Shelby) had been trying to tell Casey for years. And everything he'd been trying to tell her was now beginning to make sense.

That is, *within one's soul truly lies everything needed to be SOMEBODY.*

It's been there all the time. One needs to do nothing to earn it, and simply enough, all one has to do is believe it.

Casey was now beginning to understand this.

What she didn't understand was how. How did Pop, or Shelby, make this all happen? How did he make it all come to life for her? Truth is, she will never understand it.

Casey slowly worked her way up the wall to stand.

Before she left the alley, she opened the letter and read it one more time.

"Nobody is ever going to believe this in a million years," she said. "No way is anyone going to believe this."

≈

Every once in a while, Casey would still sit in the alley behind Buck's grocery store and think about all that had happened to her in the past few months and how much of an impact it had made on her life.

One day while sitting there deep in thought, she was suddenly interrupted by a friendly voice.

"We knew we'd find you here," a boy said.

Casey looked up. It was a few of the kids she had met at the high school she was attending this year.

"Come on," the boy said. "We're going to town. Quit sitting around and come with us."

Casey stretched out her hand.

"Help me up," she said.

The boy with red hair and a nice smile grabbed Casey's hand, gave a tug, and pulled her to her feet.

Casey steadied herself. She then paused a moment to give the boy a hard look.

"Whaaat?" the boy asked, staring back at Casey.

"Ya know," she said, "I... I still can't get over how much you look like someone I used to know."

Casey's friends looked at one another as if to say, "Aw, man. Here we go again."

"Yeah, well," the boy with red hair said as they all started to walk away, "you've told me that a million times, and before you ask me again, the answer is 'No'. I ain't never been to a place called Shelby."

There was a pause before Casey spoke up, "Nice place, Shelby is."

Casey's words echoed off the buildings in the empty alley as the group walked away.

"Nice place."

THE TEN ESSENTIAL FACTS

...A Review

1

You're going to make choices in life,
and the choices you make are going to
turn around and make you.

2

If the friends you hang out with
don't respect you *first* as a person,
chances are good that they are either
going to **USE** you or **LOSE** you.

3

We as human beings are given only
"one pair of shoes" in our lifetime
and are never allowed to walk in another.
Maybe it's time we walk in another.

4

As old fashioned as you may think it is,
commitment is the bottom line for
sexual behavior.

5

Failure is the frightful thing you see when
you take your eyes off of your goal.

6

There are two types of family problems you will
face in your life: those that you have
control over and those ***you don't***.

7

Desire
—how bad you **REALLY** want it—
is the key to success in just about anything
you do.

8

With depression, think more of yourself in terms
of getting the help you need
than you do of what others may think of you
for doing so.

9

I'd rather have ***no friends*** and do the right
thing than hang out with a hundred people
who ***use me***.

10

If you think **the *things you do***
and ***the way you look***
will help you make the friends you want,
FANTASY LAND
is the place for you.

Have any questions?

Want to talk about something in this book?

Have any problems you'd like to talk about?

You can e-mail the **author** at

uptoyou@copper.net

~

To **order more books**
go to

teenage-book.com

~

For **more information**
on the subject matter covered in this book
or on other subjects pertaining to teenagers, go to

choicesforteens.com